PhoneGap for Enterp

Master the art of building secure enterprise mobile applications using PhoneGap

Kerri Shotts

BIRMINGHAM - MUMBAI

PhoneGap for Enterprise

First published: December 2014

Production reference: 1191214

Published by Packt Publishing Ltd.
Livery Place
35 Livery Street
Birmingham B3 2PB, UK.

ISBN 978-1-78355-475-1

www.packtpub.com

Credits

Author
Kerri Shotts

Reviewers
Steve Husting
Tony Radford
Julio César Sánchez

Commissioning Editor
Kunal Parikh

Acquisition Editor
Reshma Raman

Content Development Editor
Vaibhav Pawar

Technical Editors
Veronica Fernandes
Rohith Rajan

Copy Editor
Relin Hedly

Project Coordinator
Kranti Berde

Proofreaders
Simran Bhogal
Joyce Littlejohn
Joanna McMahon

Indexer
Rekha Nair

Graphics
Disha Haria

Production Coordinator
Alwin Roy

Cover Work
Alwin Roy

About the Author

Kerri Shotts has worked with computers for nearly 25 years. Her love for technology and programming started when she was introduced to her first computer, which was a Commodore 64. She obtained a degree in computer science at college and eventually became a software test engineer. Later on, she worked as an Oracle Database Administrator for several years. Now, she owns her own company and works as a technology consultant. Kerri is responsible for creating, designing, and maintaining custom applications (both desktop and mobile), websites, graphics, and logos for her clients. She has been actively involved with PhoneGap for several years, and has written several native and hybrid applications. You can find her blog posts at http://www.photokandy.com. Kerri is also active on the Google Group for PhoneGap and Stack Overflow. When she isn't coding or writing, she enjoys photography, music, and fishkeeping. She is the author of three other books published by Packt Publishing, including *PhoneGap 3.x Mobile Application Development Hotshot*.

About the Reviewers

Steve Husting wears various hats by day, including that of a website worker, in a company that designs and manufactures radio-controlled hobby cars. By night, he writes, does calligraphy, and creates iPhone and Android apps. He posts his findings about PhoneGap app development on his blog, `http://iphonedevlog.wordpress.com`, which is focused towards beginners.

Julio César Sánchez has been a professional software developer since 2007. Over the years, he has worked with various web-related technologies. In 2010, he discovered PhoneGap and has been following the PhoneGap Google Group since then, learning, helping other developers, and even contributing with PhoneGap plugins. He spends part of his spare time developing mobile apps. Julio also writes tutorials about PhoneGap development for `http://www.phonegap.es`. You can visit his personal website (`http://www.jcesarmobile.com`), or follow him on twitter at `@jcesarmobile` to know more about him and his work.

www.PacktPub.com

Support files, eBooks, discount offers, and more

For support files and downloads related to your book, please visit www.PacktPub.com.

Did you know that Packt offers eBook versions of every book published, with PDF and ePub files available? You can upgrade to the eBook version at www.PacktPub.com and as a print book customer, you are entitled to a discount on the eBook copy. Get in touch with us at service@packtpub.com for more details.

At www.PacktPub.com, you can also read a collection of free technical articles, sign up for a range of free newsletters and receive exclusive discounts and offers on Packt books and eBooks.

https://www2.packtpub.com/books/subscription/packtlib

Do you need instant solutions to your IT questions? PacktLib is Packt's online digital book library. Here, you can search, access, and read Packt's entire library of books.

Why subscribe?

- Fully searchable across every book published by Packt
- Copy and paste, print, and bookmark content
- On demand and accessible via a web browser

Free access for Packt account holders

If you have an account with Packt at www.PacktPub.com, you can use this to access PacktLib today and view 9 entirely free books. Simply use your login credentials for immediate access.

Table of Contents

Preface

Mobile devices are virtually ubiquitous among the enterprise workforce, and employees are becoming increasingly mobile. This book discusses how the enterprise workforce can take advantage of Apache Cordova/Adobe PhoneGap applications to create cross-platform hybrid mobile applications that can serve the varied needs of the user and the enterprise.

This book will cover the various aspects of typical hybrid app architecture, from the backend database and web servers all the way to the hybrid app that resides on the employee's device. As the security of the enterprise data is paramount, a large amount of time is focused on ensuring that the communication between the backend and the user's device is secure. The book also covers how to respond to changes in network connectivity and application state.

A code package is also available for this book. Inside, you'll find a complete backend database and web server as well as a frontend hybrid application called *Tasker*. The entire project is presented as an example that you can learn from and apply to other projects. The link to the code package is given later on in this section.

What this book covers

Chapter 1, PhoneGap and Enterprise Mobility, discusses the history of Apache Cordova/ Adobe PhoneGap applications, presents reasons why Cordova/PhoneGap is a good fit for the enterprise, and how Cordova facilitates cross-platform development for Cordova and hybrid application architecture.

Chapter 2, Building the Data Store and Business Logic, introduces you to the typical backend server architecture, as well as designing the data models and business logic. You will also get introduced to *Tasker*, the demonstration app for this book.

Chapter 3, Securing PhoneGap Apps, shows the importance of ensuring the security of enterprise data. This chapter also covers backend security, general security, and issues that relate directly to Cordova/PhoneGap apps.

Chapter 4, Building the Middle Tier, discusses RESTful-like APIs and HATEOAS (Hypertext As The Engine Of Application State). A sample Node.js server is included as a demonstration of these topics, including examples of connecting to databases, executing queries, and generating appropriate responses.

Chapter 5, Communicating Between Mobile and the Middle Tier, demonstrates how to ultilize XMLHttpRequest (XHR), SSL Certificate fingerprints, and third-party Cordova/PhoneGap plugins in order to facilitate secure communication between the mobile application and the backend servers.

Chapter 6, Application Events and Storage, briefly discusses how to respond to changes in network events and application state. This chapter also introduces a third-party SQLite plugin for persistent data storage and an additional plugin to access the iOS Keychain for secure data storage.

Chapter 7, Push Notifications, covers typical Push Notification architecture, and introduces you to Boxcar.io, a service that provides an HTTP API to send pushes. It also introduces a PhoneGap API to respond to these push notifications.

Chapter 8, Building the Presentation Tier, covers many of the different patterns used to build a mobile application, including mock-up tools, various libraries and frameworks, common patterns (MVC, data binding, templates, and so on), forms and validation, and data visualization.

Appendix, Useful Resources, provides web links to resources that the reader might find useful for further learning. These are split chapterwise so that they can relate to a specific chapter in this book.

What you need for this book

In order to run the example code within the code package for this book, you'll need the following software:

- Oracle Database 11gR2 Express Edition (freely available from http://www. oracle.com/technetwork/database/database-technologies/express-edition/downloads/index-083047.html). You require a free Oracle account to download the packages or installer.

- Node.js 0.10.25 or higher (freely available from http://nodejs.org). This code has been tested on version 0.10.25.

- Oracle Instant Client 12c (freely available from `http://www.oracle.com/technetwork/database/features/instant-client/index-097480.html`). You require a free Oracle account.
- Cordova/PhoneGap 3.6 or higher (freely available from: `http://cordova.apache.org` or `http://phonegap.com`). This code has been tested on Cordova 3.6.

If you intend to build the Cordova/PhoneGap demonstrations locally on your machine, you'll also need to install the appropriate SDKs and prerequisite software. For more information, see: `http://cordova.apache.org/docs/en/edge/guide_cli_index.md.html#The%20Command-Line%20Interface`.

Who this book is for

The content of this book assumes that the reader has experience with the following:

- JavaScript (ECMAScript 5+)
- CSS3
- HTML5
- Cordova/PhoneGap 3.6+
- Some experience with Node.js or similar server software (like PHP)
- Some experience with databases (such as SQLite, MySQL, Oracle, and so on)

This book is aimed at the employee who desires to utilize (or who has been tasked with utilizing) Cordova/PhoneGap software to build mobile hybrid applications for the enterprise. As such, the book focuses on various enterprise technologies (including Oracle and Node). It also deals with a lot of security issues.

Conventions

In this book, you will find a number of styles of text that distinguish between different kinds of information. Here are some examples of these styles, and an explanation of their meaning.

Code words in text, database table names, folder names, filenames, file extensions, pathnames, dummy URLs, user input, and Twitter handles are shown as follows: "If the activity finished successfully, we call `deferred.resolve` with the value."

A block of code is set as follows:

```
function interpolate( str, context ) {
  var newStr = str;
  if ( typeof context === "undefined" ) {
    return newStr;
  }
  str.match( /\{((^\}]+)\}/g ).forEach( function ( match ) {
    var prop = match.substr( 1, match.length - 2 ).trim();
    newStr = newStr.replace( match,
      valueForKeyPath( context, prop ) );
  } );
  return newStr;
}
```

When we wish to draw your attention to a particular part of a code block, the relevant lines or items are set in bold:

```
function interpolate( str, context ) {
  var newStr = str;
  if ( typeof context === "undefined" ) {
    return newStr;
  }
  str.match( /\{((^\}]+)\}/g ).forEach( function ( match ) {
    var prop = match.substr( 1, match.length - 2 ).trim();
    newStr = newStr.replace( match,
      valueForKeyPath( context, prop ) );
  } );
  return newStr;
}
```

Any command-line input or output is written as follows:

```
cordova plugin add https://github.com/EddyVerbruggen/
SSLCertificateChecker-PhoneGap-Plugin.git
```

New terms and **important words** are shown in bold. Words that you see on the screen, in menus or dialog boxes for example, appear in the text like this: "clicking the **Next** button moves you to the next screen".

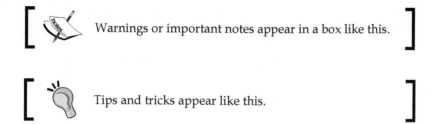

> Warnings or important notes appear in a box like this.

> Tips and tricks appear like this.

Reader feedback

Feedback from our readers is always welcome. Let us know what you think about this book—what you liked or disliked. Reader feedback is important for us as it helps us develop titles that you will really get the most out of.

To send us general feedback, simply e-mail feedback@packtpub.com, and mention the book's title in the subject of your message.

If there is a topic that you have expertise in and you are interested in either writing or contributing to a book, see our author guide at www.packtpub.com/authors.

Customer support

Now that you are the proud owner of a Packt book, we have a number of things to help you to get the most from your purchase.

Downloading the example code

You can download the example code files for all Packt books you have purchased from your account at http://www.packtpub.com. If you purchased this book elsewhere, you can visit http://www.packtpub.com/support and register to have the files e-mailed directly to you.

The code for this book is also available on GitHub at https://github.com/kerrishotts/PhoneGap-Enterprise-Code-Bundle. This repository may be updated from time to time in order to fix any errors or issues discovered.

Errata

Although we have taken every care to ensure the accuracy of our content, mistakes do happen. If you find a mistake in one of our books—maybe a mistake in the text or the code—we would be grateful if you could report this to us. By doing so, you can save other readers from frustration and help us improve subsequent versions of this book. If you find any errata, please report them by visiting http://www.packtpub. com/submit-errata, selecting your book, clicking on the **Errata Submission Form** link, and entering the details of your errata. Once your errata are verified, your submission will be accepted and the errata will be uploaded to our website or added to any list of existing errata under the Errata section of that title.

To view the previously submitted errata, go to https://www.packtpub.com/books/ content/support and enter the name of the book in the search field. The required information will appear under the **Errata** section.

Piracy

Piracy of copyright material on the Internet is an ongoing problem across all media. At Packt, we take the protection of our copyright and licenses very seriously. If you come across any illegal copies of our works, in any form, on the Internet, please provide us with the location address or website name immediately so that we can pursue a remedy.

Please contact us at copyright@packtpub.com with a link to the suspected pirated material.

We appreciate your help in protecting our authors, and our ability to bring you valuable content.

Questions

If you have a problem with any aspect of this book, you can contact us at questions@packtpub.com, and we will do our best to address the problem.

1
PhoneGap and Enterprise Mobility

The enterprise has always focused on providing solutions that enable its users to access important data in a variety of ways. With smartphones being the norm, the enterprise can leverage the mobility of its users and deliver real-time data in a timely fashion. Of course, the smartphone environment is a quickly changing and rapidly evolving environment; as such, solutions need to be equally agile.

PhoneGap/Cordova is a framework that enables the enterprise to target multiple smartphone platforms with a single code base using technologies the enterprise is already largely familiar with. It's a perfect fit for the enterprise, as it doesn't require duplication of effort to build multiple native applications that must essentially be rewritten for each supported platform. Users like choice in their mobile devices, and PhoneGap/Cordova allows the enterprise to offer just that.

Furthermore, since PhoneGap/Cordova provides developers with access to the native features of the user's mobile device, it also provides the necessary technologies to interact with the enterprise's systems over a variety of networks. This means that users can be highly mobile without losing access to highly valuable and timely enterprise data.

It is this ability of PhoneGap/Cordova to display both content using web-based technologies, and interface with the mobile device using native technologies that gives rise to the term **hybrid**. This simply means that PhoneGap/Cordova apps are neither purely web-based (as a web app would be), nor are they purely native-based (as a native iOS app would be); they are a blend of the two. This allows PhoneGap/Cordova apps to be written using technologies already established within the enterprise while also allowing immense flexibility.

In this chapter, we'll cover the following sections:

- Some history behind PhoneGap/Cordova
- Reasons why it makes perfect sense in an enterprise development
- How PhoneGap/Cordova enables fast cross-platform development
- The application structure and the technology stack

 Throughout this book, we'll often use the term "Cordova" to refer to both PhoneGap and Cordova. PhoneGap is a distribution of Cordova and is very similar to Cordova. Where there are differences, this book will mention them separately by name.

This book assumes that the reader has a good working knowledge of PhoneGap/Cordova from a personal perspective, and is also someone who is now tasked with taking that knowledge into the enterprise. As such, we won't cover the installation of PhoneGap/Cordova, neither will we cover the installation of native platform SDKs.

Why PhoneGap/Cordova?

Cordova is a natural fit for the enterprise environment for many reasons, some of which are listed as follows:

- Quickly create cross-platform hybrid apps with little duplication of work and high code reuse
- Leverage technologies already known by most developers familiar with web, multi-tier, and backend development
- Access native features on mobile hardware—including network information, device location, camera, and more
- Where necessary, create custom plugins to extend PhoneGap/Cordova for specific needs
- Embed PhoneGap/Cordova into existing native apps as a component
- A very active development community (nearly 22,000 members in the Google group for PhoneGap), including a good deal of third-party plugin development (as of this writing, 1,168 plugins are made available by 797 different authors); core development is supported by Adobe (PhoneGap) and Apache (Cordova)

- Ability to deploy apps internally or to app stores
- Open source (Apache license)
- Enterprise-grade support options available
- Additional features offered for PhoneGap by Adobe for the enterprise (`http://enterprise.phonegap.com`)

History behind PhoneGap and Cordova

Initially, PhoneGap was owned by Nitobi Software. In earlier versions, it was distributed in the form of project templates that could be used in Xcode or Eclipse to create hybrid apps. While it was easy to develop single-platform apps, it was more difficult to develop cross-platform apps (one had to create copies of the web-specific code and keep those copies synchronized across projects). Even so, many production apps were developed and hosted on app stores, and many more were developed and distributed internally within enterprises.

In 2011, Adobe purchased Nitobi Software. As part of the acquisition, the PhoneGap code was contributed to Apache and made open source. The project was ultimately renamed as Apache Cordova. Adobe kept the PhoneGap name and began maintaining a fork of Apache Cordova's code. As such, the version was changed to 2.x. Generally, the two were largely identical (with only minor variations). Since the project templates of the prior 1.x era were often problematic, the project creation transitioned to a **command-line interface (CLI)**. Cross-platform development was now somewhat easier, though not yet ideal.

Apache Cordova 3.x was released in July 2013. It provided a new CLI that dramatically simplified cross-platform development while also making plugin installation easier and less problematic than before. It also decoupled many of the core features and distributed them as core plugins instead. This allowed developers to pick and choose which plugins they needed rather than taking them out later (which was often difficult). This means that apps written with 3.x only need to ask for the permissions they actually use, whereas under 2.x, an app would often ask for permissions it never needed.

Easy cross-platform development

Since writing a native app will require an app to be rebuilt from scratch for each additional platform, in Cordova, the largest portion of the app is built on web technologies that are inherently cross-platform. Only the native wrapper and native plugins are specific to each particular platform.

In the 1.x version of PhoneGap, the developer was required to compile the project on their own development machine. The developer needed a machine capable of supporting the specific development environment for each of the supported platforms. When 2.x was released, Adobe made it possible to build projects in the cloud, and recently, they also enabled on-device testing with no build requirement at all.

This means that the developer has many different environments that they can use and none of these environments are mutually exclusive (many are used together). The environments are shown in the following diagram:

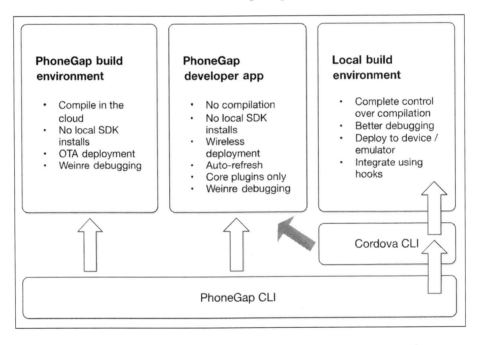

Many developers still prefer the local development environment, even though it often requires a good deal of setup and maintenance. The local build environment offers the greatest degree of control because the entire build process takes place on the developer's machine. It's also the most secure: the files and assets remain completely within the enterprise's network unless deploying the app externally.

The **PhoneGap build environment** allows developers to write their apps on their machine using a text editor and then upload these apps to the cloud for compilation. This means that there is no need to set up and maintain a full development environment—a good text editor is sufficient (though an editor that understands web development is a good idea). There are some platforms that require additional steps before the results can be tested or deployed. However, Apple for example, requires various certificates and provisioning prior to it being tested and deployed on real devices.

Recently, PhoneGap also released the PhoneGap Developer App—this app is downloadable from several app stores and provides one more way to test apps on real devices. The app is itself a PhoneGap app that can connect to your development machine to load HTML, CSS, and JavaScript code. Furthermore, it includes all the core plugins, and if these are all that an app requires, the app can be tested on a physical device without any compilation at all. (Of course, if third-party or custom plugins are necessary, this is no longer entirely possible.) Furthermore, any changes to the code are automatically reflected on the device, eliminating the tedious build and deploy cycle. (This app also works with the Cordova CLI without automatic reloading.) From the security perspective, the app works only on a local network, and unlike PhoneGap Build, no files or assets are transmitted externally.

Ultimately, the result of the Cordova/PhoneGap CLI and the various build environments is to make cross-platform development easier, and enable faster and more agile development (this in turn enables the enterprise to become far more mobile than ever before). Although there is still some native code available that is specific to each platform (including the wrapper around the app's HTML, CSS, and JavaScript and any additional plugins), the CLI makes managing these bits simple, and lets the developer focus on writing the truly cross-platform HTML, CSS, and JavaScript code.

The following diagram shows a simplified view of how this looks:

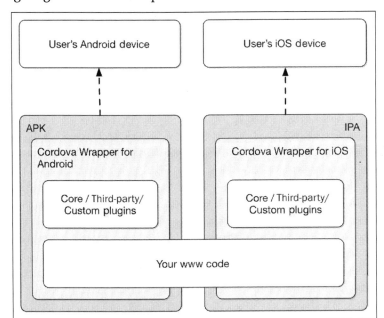

Cordova app architecture

The WWW or web code is inherently cross-platform (assuming web standards are followed) and should be the same on all platforms. Where necessary, different code paths can be built for specific devices, though this is usually only necessary when talking to certain third-party plugins that are specific to certain platforms.

This cross-platform web code is wrapped by native code. This code is specific to each platform the app supports (and so the app can only run on platforms supported by Cordova). This native code serves to bootstrap the app and instantiate a single full-screen system browser in which the web code is executed.

The native code initializes any native plugins as well; these can be core plugins provided by the Cordova team, third-party plugins developed by other members in the community, or custom plugins developed internally by the enterprise. This is a major benefit of using Cordova; if a particular feature isn't best handled or possible using web technologies, there can be a plugin developed by someone else that implements this feature. If there isn't such a plugin available, it's usually pretty easy to create such a plugin internally.

The native code also provides a **bridge**, or **interface**, between the native plugins and platform, and the web code. This bridge provides the mechanism by which the web code can access native device features by providing a simple and consistent API. This enables a web code to talk to specific plugins in order to perform native device functions.

The following diagram provides a bird's-eye view of how each layer talks to one another:

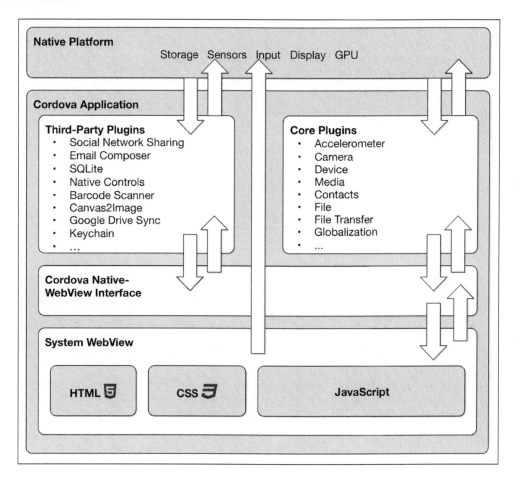

Cordova app structure

A typical Cordova app has the following structure on the filesystem:

```
Project/
    config.xml   — project settings, description, etc.
    build.shl*   — your project's build script
    readme.md*   — your project's information
    ...          — any other project-specific files

    www/ — JavaScript, HTML, and CSS files specific to your project (as well as any
    frameworks, libraries, etc.)
        for example:
        css/
        html/
        js/
            app/
            lib/
        index.html

    hooks/ — Optional project-specific hooks which allow you to inject your own
    process into the Cordova/PhoneGap CLI (for example: integration with your build
    server)

    merges/ — Platform-specific JavaScript, HTML, and CSS files (optional)
        ios/
        android/

    platforms/ — native code projects (exclude from source repository)

    plugins/ — installed plugins (exclude from source repository)
```

A typical Cordova project has a `config.xml` file in the root directory of the project that specifies the name, description, and other attributes for the project. There can be other files (such as a build script or a `readme` file, indicated by an asterisk in the previous diagram) that are also project-specific and internally developed by the enterprise to support the project. (If you want to see examples of these additional files, feel free to look at the code package for this book.)

Downloading the example code

You can download the example code files for all Packt books you have purchased from your account at http://www.packtpub.com. If you purchased this book elsewhere, you can visit http://www.packtpub.com/support and register to have the files e-mailed directly to you.

All of the web code is put in the root www directory. There are other www directories in other various subdirectories (in the platforms directory); however, these are all duplicates and should be considered build artifacts (they are overwritten each time the project is built). As such, don't commit the platforms directory to your **Version Control System (VCS)**.

The structure of the root www directory is specific to the project under development, and the various frameworks and libraries being used. The example in the preceding diagram is a portion of my typical directory structure within the www directory. Ultimately, there is neither a preferred nor mandated structure within this directory.

The hooks directory might not exist, and it should only be used if you need to perform custom actions when specific events occur in the project. For example, you might need to create a hook that notifies an external build system that the app's build was successful; such a hook will be created in this directory.

 Hooks are beyond the scope of this book as they are highly specific to each enterprise and app. However, there is a lot of information available online. The documentation at https://github.com/apache/cordova-lib/blob/master/cordova-lib/templates/hooks-README.md would be a good starting point.

The merges directory is another directory that might not exist and it should be avoided if at all possible. The original intent was to provide a way to override code in the www directory with platform-specific www code. If this code is correctly written according to the various web standards, then it is rarely necessary to use this functionality. If your app needs to behave differently on different devices, it is better to detect the device and branch appropriately.

The platforms directory includes every platform added to the project. As new platforms are added, native wrappers are created within this folder, and the www directory gets duplicated within these wrappers. Essentially, one should consider this directory a build artifact and it should never be checked into VCS.

The plugins directory includes every plugin added to the project. Similar to the platforms directory, it should be considered a build artifact and should never be checked into your VCS. The plugin management should instead be managed using the CLI or a shell script. If you want a good example, please check out the code package for this book.

None of this details how the www code should be structured or what architecture it should use. Cordova is not prescriptive in this regard — you can leverage your knowledge of the existing web frameworks (such as jQuery, Sencha Touch, and so on) and other libraries (such as Underscore, Backbone.js, and so on).

Summary

In this chapter, we introduced you to PhoneGap/Cordova and a little bit of its history. We covered the various environments you can use to develop a Cordova app. We also briefly touched upon the application's architecture. Finally, we covered the typical application structure used to create Cordova apps. Before moving on, you might want to visit *Appendix A, More about PhoneGap/Cordova*, which lists many sites that contain more information regarding PhoneGap and Cordova.

In the next chapter, we'll cover designing and implementing the business logic for your enterprise app built in PhoneGap/Cordova.

2
Building the Data Store and Business Logic

Enterprise apps, by their very nature, require a data store that is capable of persisting data and business logic that manipulates data. This can be comprised of any number of technologies, though there are usually several servers involved, including database, application, and authentication servers.

In this chapter, we'll cover the following topics:

- Typical server architecture
- Designing data models
- Writing business logic and where that logic should be placed
- Designing permissions and authorization models
- An introduction to Tasker, our demonstration app

Of course, it's impossible to cover all of these topics extensively in the next few pages. As such, if you need to create a large system from scratch, including the business logic and data models, you might want to do quite a bit of research into the various tools and technologies that you might want to use. Above all, *use the right tools for the job*—just because we use certain technologies in our demonstration app, it does not mean that you must use them in your own app. Instead, research your technologies carefully and use the ones that best meet your needs.

The code package for this book contains design documents and SQL code that this chapter touches upon. You will probably want to download the code package and have it handy as we progress through the chapter. The code package is also available on GitHub at `https://github.com/kerrishotts/PhoneGap-Enterprise-Code-Bundle`. The backend code and business logic lives within the `database` directory in this bundle.

Introducing Tasker

I find having an example useful when learning about technology, and this book is no exception. The code package for this book contains an example enterprise application representing each of the following four tiers: the database, business logic, web service API, and presentation layer.

Tasker is intentionally designed to be a very simple app, far simpler than many enterprise apps. This isn't a bad thing; it enables us to worry about the critical issues related to enterprise app development without having a complex application that defies understanding. Instead, Tasker is largely what it sounds like: a simple task management app.

Of course, a to-do list doesn't sound very enterprise-y. As such, Tasker isn't about managing a single task list, but about managing and delegating many tasks to many users. The app is built with the idea that the entire organization will be using this app to track their work. As such, tasks are owned by their creator, and they can also be assigned to other individuals. The owner or the assignee can update the task status or add comments as well. Finally, individuals can only see the tasks they are assigned or the tasks that they own, which adds a level of security.

Server architecture

Although Tasker is a simple app, we've built it to mirror a typical enterprise setup, as shown in the following diagram:

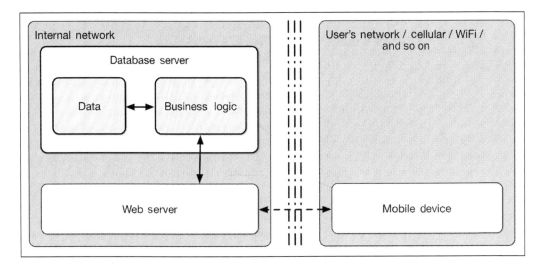

The mobile device (say, the user's phone) is considered the **presentation tier** of the app; this is where the data is displayed to the user and where they can manipulate it. Although this book is a PhoneGap book, we actually won't deal with this tier until *Chapter 5, Communicating between Mobile and the Middle Tier*, and later, since we need to establish the foundation of the app first.

The mobile device doesn't have to live on the enterprise's network. Depending on the sensitivity of the data, the mobile device might be expected to connect to the enterprise's network using a **Virtual Private Network** (**VPN**). This essentially means that the device exists within the enterprise's network. Since this adds an extra burden on the user (they need to connect to the VPN prior to using the app), this isn't always desirable. For this reason, we've built our app under the assumption that our app won't require a VPN.

> There's no real difference in how we code our app whether or not we connect to the backend using a VPN. It largely boils down to how much we trust the intervening networks with the data we are handling, and the trade-off for the end user when managing the VPN connection. The code, however, operates in the same way.

The dotted lines in the preceding diagram represent the dividing line between the Internet and the user's network and the enterprise's internal network. All communication comes into the web server, which represents the **web service API** for our app. The web server receives requests from the presentation layer and then passes them on to the database server, which represents the **backend** or **data tier** of the app. In our case, the data tier also contains a good deal of the **logic tier** (where calculations are made and data is manipulated).

Since Tasker's logic lives in the database, the actual architecture looks more like the following diagram:

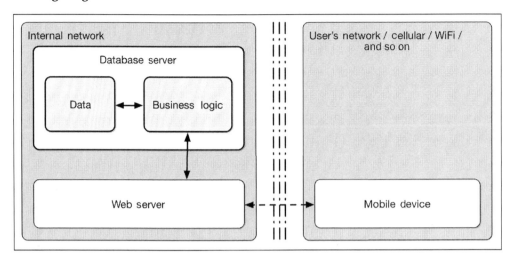

Regardless of the architecture, it is important to note that the database server has no direct exposure to the outside world. At the minimum, the database server will be placed behind the enterprise's firewall. It's also not uncommon for many firewalls to be used in order to create various zones of ever-increasing security.

Even though the database server's exposure to the outside world is minimized, one must always take care to sanitize any incoming data in case a malicious user attempts to send data that will adversely affect the system. For example, SQL injection attacks are often used to inject malicious code into the database in an attempt to extract and/or destroy data.

Access to the database server must be carefully managed and protected. Should an attacker gain unauthorized access to the server, the data should be considered to be compromised — even if that data is encrypted (it just might take a while to decrypt).

Encryption is important; however, this doesn't guarantee that an attacker won't eventually gain access to the encrypted data. This is why you should never store any data that isn't necessary and also why it is important to follow security best practices. For example, don't store passwords in a form that can be decrypted; use salted hashes instead, and use a strong hashing algorithm (like **PBKDF2**). Better yet, delegate authentication to a server specifically designed for secure authentication. For example, when dealing with credit card information, avoid storing credit card numbers at any cost. Instead, delegate this responsibility to third-party providers. Your enterprise surely doesn't want to incur the cost and loss of trust, should that kind of information be leaked.

In this chapter, we're dealing with the database server. As we've mentioned, we've elected to build the business logic in the database server as well—though other enterprise apps might need to have the business logic in a separate instance. Both options are valid, and there are benefits and detriments to both methods.

For the database server itself, I've chosen Oracle 11gR2 XE on a CentOS 6.5 64-bit Linux server. The database software is a no-cost version of Oracle's Standard and Enterprise database servers that provides a simple install on many popular operating systems (Windows and Linux). The free version can store up to 11 GB of data, uses only one CPU core, and can only address 1 GB of RAM. XE doesn't support some of the same enterprise-level features that the Standard and Enterprise editions do, but for simple apps, the XE version offers an excellent trade-off between the power of an Oracle database and the cost. If you'd like to learn more about Oracle Database Express, visit `http://www.oracle.com/us/products/database/enterprise-edition/comparisons/index.html`. In fact, it isn't uncommon that XE is run in tandem with its enterprise cousins in the organization, simply due to cost and easy setup. If an app isn't storing extremely sensitive data and doesn't need a great deal of enterprise features, then an XE instance can be more cost-effective than purchasing a costlier license.

Of course, there's no reason why another database server wouldn't work. MySQL, MariaDB, PostgreSQL, SQL Server, and so on, would all have been more than sufficient for our needs, and they are sufficient for many enterprise-level apps as well. It's wise to compare the feature sets of the database servers and the needs of your app, and select the database server that will best meet the needs of the enterprise and the app.

Finally, it's critical to understand that we can't cover how to set up a database for an enterprise-level app (especially with regard to high availability, disaster recovery, table-level encryption, and so on) mainly because these are *database administrator* and *network security* concerns, and require a good deal of understanding to correctly implement. Alternatively, if you want a secure backend in the cloud that takes care of a good portion of the security side for you, you might want to consider a **Backend-as-a-Service (BaaS)** such as Parse; however, this will depend on your enterprise's willingness to have data stored in the cloud.

 Don't assume that you need a typical SQL-based database! There are lots of other options available for data persistence, including the popular NoSQL trend. For example, a document store would likely be more appropriate for a document management app. To learn more about NoSQL, see `http://en.wikipedia.org/wiki/NoSQL`.

One of the benefits of using Oracle is that it has a very expressive procedural language called PL/SQL, which makes it possible to build the app's business logic within the database. This has a benefit in that the code is available to any client connecting to the database, which is useful for reporting solutions, automated processes, and so on.

On the other hand, having the business logic in the database has a corresponding downside. The code is not necessarily portable to other platforms, and PL/SQL doesn't have the same large community that other languages have (such as Java, C, or even Objective C).

Oracle isn't the only database environment to support a procedural language, either. A SQL Server has its own flavor (Transact-SQL), as does PostgreSQL (PL/pgSQL). Even though these attempt to solve similar problems, it is not typically possible to move the code back and forth without large changes to the code – this is something you definitely must consider; is your enterprise willing to be tied to a single database server vendor or does your enterprise need to be extremely flexible with regard to database server vendors?

You'll need to weigh the advantages and disadvantages to host the business logic on the database server or on a separate instance based upon the kind of app you are building.

	Advantages	Disadvantages
Business logic in a database server	• Code is close to the data • Code is available to every consumer, such as a report server or automated process • Can be enforced at the data level • Often optimized for the data by the database server itself	• Requires coding in a programming language that fewer people are familiar with • Less portable to other database servers; changing to a different database will require rewriting the logic
Business logic in a separate instance	• Can be built using a more familiar programming language • Easily portable to other systems as long as the programming language is available (or a transpiler is available) • Separation of concerns: data and code are kept completely separate	• Code is further away from the data • Logic often needs to be rewritten for each consumer (reporting tool, automation, and so on) • Can't be enforced at the data level • May require additional effort to get good performance on large datasets

Don't want to install database server software on your own machine? Consider using a virtual machine. It will be slower than a dedicated hardware; however, it means that you don't have to risk your primary computer's configuration by installing large complicated software on your primary operating system. Alternatively, consider spinning up virtual servers on other hardware or in the cloud (be careful with security concerns if using the latter).

Designing your data models

It is important that you identify the data models your app will need prior to writing any code. Consider your data models the foundation of your app as a whole. We don't have sufficient space in this chapter to cover all the various complexities a large data model design needs to address. Instead, we'll discuss some basic ideas and also explain our mindset while going through the design for Tasker.

Simply, a data model describes the kind of data your app will store as well as the relationships between the data elements. Having this in place makes it easy to understand the system and makes it easier to code the app.

Let's go through the data models for our app. First up, we have the PERSON model:

PERSON		
ID	NUMBER	
USER_ID	VARCHAR2(32)	User ID
FIRST_NAME	VARCHAR2(255)	
MIDDLE_NAME	VARCHAR2(255)	
LAST_NAME	VARCHAR2(255)	
ADMINISTRATOR_ID	NUMBER	Link to administrator
CHANGE_DATE	DATE	
CHANGE_USER	VARCHAR2(32)	
create_person (from_user_id, first_name, middle_name, last_name)		
assign_administrator (administrator_ID, to_person)		
update_avatar_for_person (ID, avatar)		
get_people_administered_by (ID)		

The preceding diagram tells us quite a bit about the data we're storing:

- The model stores information about people, including their name and administrator

- The model indicates the data types for the individual data elements

- The model also indicates the various actions that can be performed on the data

The preceding diagram doesn't tell us much about how the data elements relate to each other (or to other models). You can probably guess that an administrator ID points at another person's ID; however, it is always better to make this explicit. We could do this on the same diagram, or use another diagram to make this clear:

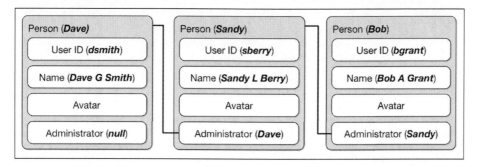

As you can tell, the PERSON data model forms a hierarchy of people who manage other people. We can also reverse this relationship to determine who manages any individual in the database. So we can ask "who is Bob's manager?" as well as "who does Sandy manage?" This is key for our permissions model (where individuals should only see tasks they own or are assigned to, and individuals can only assign tasks to those they manage).

Let's look at another data model: the TASK model. This model stores the data related to each task; information such as the title, the description, who created the task and who is assigned to it, and so on, as shown in the following diagram:

TASK		
ID	NUMBER	
TITLE	VARCHAR2(255)	
DESCRIPTION	VARCHAR2(4000)	
PCT_COMPLETE	NUMBER	% completed
STATUS	VARCHAR2(1)	(I)n-progress, (C)omplete, (H)old, (X)Deleted
OWNER	NUMBER	Link to owning Person
ASSIGNED_TO	NUMBER	Link to assigned
CHANGE_DATE	DATE	
CHANGE_USER	VARCHAR2(32)	
create_task (title, description, owned_by, assigned_to)		
update_task_percentage (ID, percentage)		
update_task_status (ID, status)		
get_tasks (owned_by, assigned_to , with_status] [, with_completion_low, with_completion_high])		

The preceding diagram should be reasonably self-explanatory; all the fields you would expect for simple task management are here. The OWNER and ASSIGNED_TO fields point to the PERSON records so we can track ownership and assignments.

 If we were building a fully extensible system, it's probable that one would actually create an additional model to store status types which would allow you to handle additional statuses instead of the four defined earlier.

The following diagram shows how a task is owned and assigned:

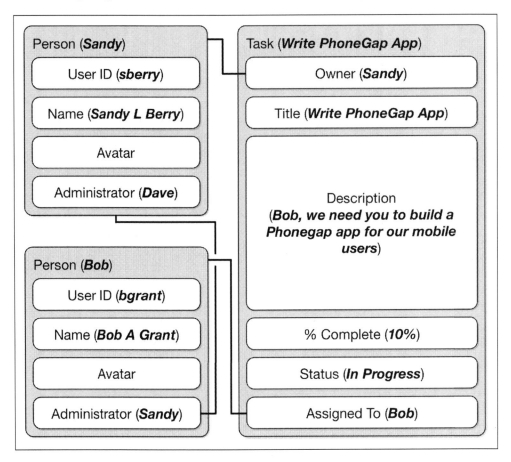

This is technically sufficient for simple task management, but it would be nice if there were a mechanism to track communication between the owner and assignee. For this feature, let's define a `TASK_COMMENTS` model:

TASK_COMMENTS		
ID	NUMBER	
TASK	NUMBER	Link to owning Task
AUTHOR	NUMBER	Link to person
COMMENTS	VARCHAR2(4000)	
CHANGE_DATE	DATE	
CHANGE_USER	VARCHAR2(32)	
create_task_comment (task_ID, comment)		
get_comments_for_task (task_ID)		

This model allows us to store any number of comments per task. Later on, we'll use this model to enable the addition of push notifications to our mobile app.

The following diagram should make the relationship between tasks and comments easier to see:

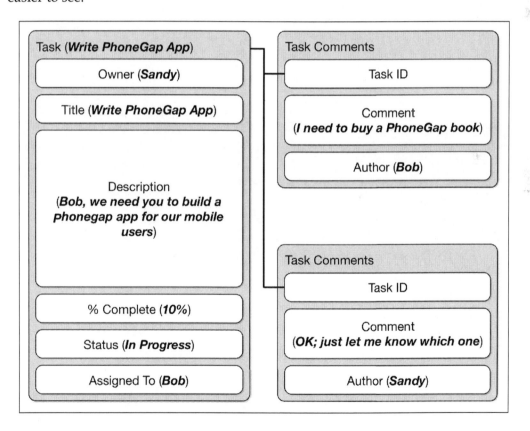

As you can see in the preceding diagram, it's possible to have more than one comment per task.

Typically relationships are expressed in a data model diagram by connecting lines between the two models (and indicating if the relationship is one-to-one, one-to-many, many-to-many, and so on). In our case, compressing the entire diagram to fit on a page is hard to read, so we've left these connecting lines out in the preceding diagrams. The following is an example of what this looks like as a whole:

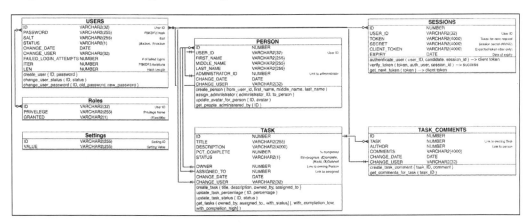

When creating data models, the following concepts might be useful:

- Models represent physical objects; for example, our PERSON model represents a real person. In the database, a model is often a table of data.

- Data elements represent attributes or properties of the model. A person has a name and an administrator, which are described in the model as individual fields. In the database, a data element is often a column within a table.

- Relationships can be one-to-one, one-to-many, and many-to-many. A person can have only one administrator, but an administrator can have many subordinates (one-to-many). On the other hand, a person has only one username (one-to-one). Furthermore, relationships can be optional or required; for example, a task must be owned by a person, but might not be assigned to another individual.

This is, of course, extremely condensed. If you want to learn more about designing data models, see the *Designing the data models* section in *Appendix, Useful Resources*.

Designing the business logic

When designing your business logic, it is important to think about how your app will need to access your data and what operations it will need to perform. We've defined many of these as part of the data models in the prior data model diagrams — these are the actions that our app can perform on the data. Generally this logic is pretty simple — nearly all of it boils down to something as follows:

- Retrieve (SELECT) data from tables
- Add (INSERT) data into tables
- Update (UPDATE) data in tables
- Remove (DELETE) data from tables
- Return data back to the app

We won't take up valuable space in this chapter by including all the code for the business logic — it's pretty boring. Instead, look at the database directory in the code package for this book. Also, note that the backend database was designed to be simple and easy to understand; the design we use is not the most secure model. Data, views, and stored procedures are usually separated into separate schemas, and permissions and rights are usually assigned based on the user that is logged in to the database.

Permissions model

When it comes to data security, there are usually several tiers. Of course, one wants to secure where the data lives and the transmission of that data; however, most enterprise apps need some level of data permissions as well, that is, certain users should only be able to see certain data or certain users should only be permitted to do certain manipulations.

Tasker's permissions model is inherently simple: every person is a user of the system, and every user can create tasks. Tasks can only be *modified* by their owner. Users can also manage other users, meaning that users can assign tasks to their subordinates. When a task is assigned to another individual, the assignee can update certain fields, namely progress and status. Both the owner and assignee can add comments to a task.

Of course, this doesn't cover the authentication and authorization or user administration mechanism, and that's by design. Many enterprises will have their own requirements when it comes to authentication and authorization; there will often be servers that can handle the authorization for you within the enterprise. As such, we've not dealt with this here. The code package has a very rudimentary system just to make it all work, but if you have the option, you should never reimplement authentication and authorization on your own. If you have the choice, use a product specially made to handle authentication and authorization (LDAP, Active Directory, and so on) or a well-vetted framework (OAuth, and so on) and follow the security recommendations that the system suggests.

Summary

In this chapter, we briefly introduced Tasker, our example application. We went through the system architecture and the database server we are using. We described the data models in more detail, namely PERSON, TASK, and TASK_COMMENTS, as well as how the data relates to other data. We mentioned the business logic; this is in the code package for the book, but it's all self-explanatory, so we didn't include any code in the text. Finally, we covered the permissions model for the app.

Chances are good that you might not have to worry about how to create data models, writing business logic, or designing a complete system architecture since a lot of this might be done for you (more likely in a larger enterprise). If you do have to design your own models and logic, you might want to refer to the *Designing the data models* section in *Appendix, Useful Resources*.

In the next chapter we'll cover some important security aspects when it comes to building Cordova apps and web services.

3
Securing PhoneGap Apps

As with any application (whether single-tier or multi-tier), security is absolutely critical. Although it's tempting to dig in and start developing the next killer app right away, it's also important to build a good security framework prior to additional development. Otherwise, it's likely that one will miss a security hole or the developer will have to rewrite code in order to fix any security issues.

It is also important to recognize that no developer is perfect; it is vital that your code undergoes many code reviews by many different developers (something typical of open source projects). However, it's also true that should the code base be subjected to many eyes and code reviews, security holes and other issues will still manage to make it through to the final project. Thinking about security prior to writing code can go a long way to ensure a good foundation, but it can't ensure that your product is completely secure.

There's a fine line we walk when giving our app to the user: the user has to run our code, but we also have to protect ourselves against the malicious user who might use that same code against us. For example, your app might need to store sensitive data on the device, but this device is in the user's control. This means that, with enough time and initiative, the user can almost certainly crack the code and gain access. A good deal of security is often the trade-off between the difficulty of implementation, the penalty a non-malicious user might pay for the security, and how much time and effort you think an attacker will spend to crack your app.

In this chapter, we won't be writing a lot of code just yet, this is about building a good foundation on how to write our code. We'll cover the following topics:

- General security precautions
    - Filtering and validating input
    - Encoding and escaping output

- ° JavaScript/browser security
  - ° Avoiding JavaScript cryptography in the browser
  - ° Avoiding the use of JavaScript `eval`
  - ° Using Strict mode
  - ° Avoiding untrusted HTML injection
  - ° Using Strict-Transport-Security
  - ° Securing your cookies
  - ° Using Content-Security-Policy
  - ° Avoiding JSONP
  - ° Avoiding the use of `iframes`
- ° Using TLS/SSL always
- ° Authentication

- • Server-specific security precautions
  - ° Securing your backend
  - ° Hardening your backend against attack
    - ° Avoiding SQL injection
    - ° Preventing cross-site request forgeries
    - ° Avoid trusting your client's state
    - ° Verify message integrity with HMACs
  - ° Quick Node.js and Express server security settings

- • Cordova-specific security precautions
  - ° Targeting modern mobile devices
  - ° Source code protection
  - ° Using InAppBrowser for external links
  - ° Whitelisting domains
  - ° Avoiding self-signed certificates
  - ° Using a well-known certificate authority
  - ° Man-in-the-middle attacks
  - ° Local data store security/encryption

General security precautions

Although this book is focused on building a secure Cordova app, many of the following security concepts apply to most situations, including native and web apps. We can't cover every possible security risk, but the following should give you a good foundation.

Filtering and validating input

It's tempting to think that the data coming from any of your app's tiers will be safe to use; after all, the data has been entered by your enterprise's users, and it's been passed through code you've written.

Unfortunately, not every user in your enterprise will always enter safe data as no one is perfect. Furthermore, if a malicious user gained access to your app (or any of the middle or backend tiers), they will certainly send malicious data in an attempt to compromise your system.

There are many different kinds of unsafe input and you've probably heard about some of these attacks in the news, including SQL and code injection, and buffer overruns. **SQL injection** relies on poorly constructed database queries. Malicious input can leak data to the attacker or such input can delete or corrupt data within your database, or both. **Code injection**, enables an attacker to run arbitrary code within your app, meaning their code will have the same privileges your code has. A buffer overrun, on the other hand, is when an attacker sends your app too much data. This data usually contains code that is designed to execute, should the app try and store the data in a buffer that isn't large enough. This can cause any number of problems (the least of which is data corruption).

Not all input is designed to be malicious; in many cases, it is simply troublesome. Because hybrid mobile apps display their content using HTML, it will be possible for the malformed input to corrupt the DOM tree. For example, if a user inserted a less-than (<) sign or a greater-than (>) sign and your code didn't filter this correctly, it might be possible for the browser to interpret this at the start (or end) of an HTML tag, potentially corrupting your app's visuals.

Finally, always ensure that your code verifies that incoming data is of the right type and length. For numbers, ensure that the input is within the expected range. If a field only supports specific values, make sure that you don't allow a value that isn't valid.

Encoding and escaping output

It's also critical that you encode and escape your output properly. This is essentially the corollary to the previous section. Just as you shouldn't trust data coming from the user, your app shouldn't implicitly trust that the data coming from the backend won't be malformed. As such, you should always attempt to encode this data when displaying it so that it can't have an undesired impact. For example, let's imagine the following code:

```
var x = {
  name: document.getElementById("name").value
};
```

Now let's imagine you want to render this object using JSON but don't know about `JSON.stringify`. You might do this:

```
return '{ "name": "' + x.name + '"}';
```

You might be inclined to think that this is good until someone enters a name that contains a double quote instead of an apostrophe (such as O"Connor). At this point, this code returns invalid JSON of this form:

```
{ "name": "O"Connor" }
```

While it's easy for humans to ignore the mismatched quotes, a computer won't. This will almost certainly result in unwanted and undesired behaviors.

Luckily, it's easy to fix this kind of error. You can, for example, choose to escape the single quotes:

```
return '{ "name": "' + x.name.replace('"','\\\"') + '"}';
```

A better solution in this case, of course, would be to use `JSON.stringify` as it handles escaping your data automatically:

```
return JSON.stringify(x);
```

JavaScript/browser security

JavaScript was originally designed to be easy for beginners to learn. While this goal is laudable, there were many decisions made when designing the language that make it all too easy to shoot oneself in the foot. It's all too simple to write a code that is susceptible to all manner of attacks, including **cross-site scripting** (**XSS**) attacks. These attacks are JavaScript code injection attacks. If the app doesn't properly filter user input or fails in properly sandboxing the external content, the injected code can be executed.

The same also applies to the browser. The browser is extremely complicated and is susceptible to any number of attacks. Because the browser is a hybrid app's renderer, this presents a large attack surface. For example, one attack vector might be a specially crafted image that takes advantage of a browser bug, thus enabling the code embedded in the image to execute in the browser.

We can't cover every risk, but we can go over a few of the high-level ones that immediately improve your security.

Avoiding JavaScript cryptography in the browser

There are tremendous difficulties in implementing cryptography using JavaScript in the browser environment for the following reasons:

- JavaScript is easily readable. Any attempt to obfuscate JavaScript requires publishing the code to de-obfuscate your code, which means a malicious attacker can easily regenerate the original code. It's also easy to gain access to any encryption keys or secrets that are stored in the code.

- The JavaScript environment is highly malleable. While this makes JavaScript very flexible, it also makes it very difficult to control the actual environment in which the code runs. Cryptography requires a verified and stable environment, otherwise the results are potentially insecure.

- JavaScript is slow. If you need to do cryptography, do it natively so that you'll get much better performance. Many cryptography methods require a large number of iterations in order to be secure. Performing these iterations natively can allow you to perform more iterations in a shorter period of time than the equivalent JavaScript code. For example, PBKDF2 is a password hashing method that needs a significant number of iterations in order to be secure (in the order of nearly one hundred thousand). Even the best browser on the fastest desktop can't perform such a computation without pausing for a significantly longer time in comparison to native code. Although PBKDF2 is designed to be slow, your users will have limited patience and they probably will not wait for several minutes to compute a password hash.

 There's a very good article available online at: `http://matasano.com/articles/javascript-cryptography/`. When you have some free time, you should go read it for full effect; it deals with this topic in much more detail.

Why does this matter? It's tempting to try and do cryptography and encryption in your JavaScript code; after all, it's where the rest of your code lives. It's natural to avoid native code as much as possible in order to ensure that the maximum amount of code is cross-platform by default.

In the browser, JavaScript cryptography is far too easy to bypass and render ineffective. If you must do any form of cryptography, push it to native code along with any sensitive secrets (that is, don't store a secret in JavaScript!). Native code isn't invulnerable, but doing this in JavaScript is hopeless.

 It's typical for web services to require requests to be signed using a secret key. The signing is usually done with **SHA256**. This is one area where you can use JavaScript in the browser as long as you retrieve the signing secret from the server (rather than hardcoding or storing it). This isn't invulnerable, of course, but request signing isn't intended to offer a lot of security. Request signing is instead intended to be a way to verify the integrity of the message (that is, checking if the message has been corrupted or altered). If you have to sign a lot of requests quickly or sign large requests, you might still wish to do this natively as even SHA256 in JavaScript is quite slow. For a few small requests, JavaScript is sufficient. Whatever you do, though, do not store the secret on the client, as that would be easy to compromise.

Avoiding the use of JavaScript eval

JavaScript allows you to use `eval` for dynamic evaluation, as follows:

```
var x = eval("2 + 2");
```

Now, imagine if anyone ever managed to insert their own code into your `eval` method, their code will run with the same privileges as your own. Using HTML5 or `use strict;` doesn't protect you much either in this particular case.

Even if you feel you must absolutely have `eval`, it's best to avoid it. Even if you know what you're doing, it's very easy to introduce a huge security hole into your app when using `eval`. Better to stay away completely.

This applies to any method by which you can inject code using strings. The `eval` method isn't the only method that can be attacked in this way; `setTimeout`, `setInterval`, `new Function`, inline event listeners (such as `onclick`), and so on, can all take strings as arguments and can all be attacked. The `eval` method is one of the worst offenders, but it really boils down to this: never execute any data as code, period. Code in strings is never code: it's data and should be treated as such. Failure to do so will only cause major headaches.

It wasn't uncommon a long time ago to use `eval` to parse JSON, but this was a bad idea for all the reasons mentioned previously. Now there's no reason to use `eval` in this case, use `JSON.parse` instead.

Using strict mode

Strict mode changes a few things when it comes to typical JavaScript behavior. Where code might otherwise fail silently, strict mode fails loudly. Strict mode also adjusts how `eval` works, but it fails making it much more secure. So, you should still avoid using `eval`.

You can apply strict mode on a file basis or a function basis, depending on your needs or the needs of any frameworks your code relies on. Not all code works under strict mode (especially older code), but any code segments that don't should be clearly called out and audited to ensure that there is no risk.

Using strict mode is simple; just put it at the head of your file or function as follows:

```
"use strict";
```

Avoiding untrusted HTML injection

`innerHTML` doesn't become dangerous until you pass untrusted data. This means that if you have a hardcoded string that never changes, it's safe to use `innerHTML`. As an example, it's common to assign an empty string to `innerHTML` as a fast way to remove all the children from a given DOM element. However, when you pass untrusted data, `innerHTML` becomes a minefield.

 It's a common tactic to use `innerHTML` when one needs to insert arbitrary HTML into the DOM element. HTML is painful to embed within JavaScript strings, but it's seen as more complicated to use the DOM element creation and management methods (such as `createElement` and `appendChild`).

`innerHTML` has a particularly nasty feature: in some browsers, it will allow execution of code in any element's event handler, which makes this as risky as `eval`. For example:

```
var name = document.getElementById("name").value,
html = "<div>" + name + "</div>";
someElement.innerHTML = html;
```

This looks innocuous until you consider what happens if the user enters `<img src='/' onload="alert(1);" />` into the `name` field. This code is run with the same privileges as your own, meaning that it could easily compromise your entire system.

In HTML5, the specification makes it clear that `innerHTML` won't evaluate script tags; so if you aren't using HTML5 this is a good reason to start. Unfortunately, it's still possible to evaluate arbitrary JavaScript code using event handlers.

`innerHTML` isn't the only vulnerable method. The following should also be avoided:

- `innerText`
- `insertAdjacentHTML`
- `document.write/document.writeln`

Although convenient, especially with regard to templating, it's simply safer to avoid their use altogether. Use the `textContent` property instead, which is incapable of running any code that might be contained within the untrusted data and is also incapable of inserting untrusted HTML content. For templating, use compiled templates or use the DOM methods (`appendChild`, `createElement`, for example) exclusively.

Using Strict-Transport-Security

It would be nice to ensure that the browser can always access your resources using **SSL/TLS**. To let the browser know that it should only access your content using a secure channel, you can set the `Strict-Transport-Security` HTTP header (either from your server or in a `META` tag) as follows:

```
Strict-Transport-Security: max-age=1234567; includeSubDomains
```

The `max-age` parameter ensures that the browser will remember your request to serve content via SSL/TLS and no other method for the specified length of time (measured in seconds). The second parameter is optional, but if supplied, it indicates that the same should be true for any subdomains. This means that, if a later attempt to access the resource does not make use of `https`, the browser will automatically use SSL/TLS anyway.

 Note: Using `strict-transport-security` will also prevent the connection should the certificate be invalid.

Unfortunately, not every mobile browser understands this header; however, for the ones that do, it's wise to have it in place to make your app much more secure. To keep up to date on browser support for this header, see `http://caniuse.com/stricttransportsecurity`.

Securing your cookies

Because cookies often contain session information, it's best to ensure that they are protected. You can set the `Secure` attribute on a cookie to ensure that it can only be sent over SSL. You should also set the `HttpOnly` attribute so that JavaScript code can't physically interact with the cookie (with `document.cookie`, for example).

How you configure your application server to send secure cookies is dependent on your web server. For common servers, OWASP has further information at: `https://www.owasp.org/index.php/SecureFlag` and `https://www.owasp.org/index.php/HttpOnly`.

If you're sending cookies via an HTTP header, use the following code (see `https://www.owasp.org/index.php/HttpOnly` for more information):

```
Set-Cookie: <name>=<value>[; <Max-Age>=<age>]
[; expires=<date>][; domain=<domain_name>]
[; path=<some_path>]; secure; HttpOnly
```

Using Content-Security-Policy

The `Content-Security-Policy` HTTP header makes XSS attacks more difficult by eliminating several of the common attack vectors, such as inline event handlers (for example, `onclick`), eval (and similar) code, and all JavaScript URLs (`href="javascript:alert(1)"`).

The header allows you to control the origins that are trusted for specific types of content. You can specify, for example, the fonts that can be allowed from external hosts, while scripts should only be allowed from your own server.

The form is as follows:

```
Content-Security-Policy: policy
```

Where policy is any combination of the following items and the allowed hosts (separated with semicolons):

- `default-src`: This applies to all content types unless otherwise overridden explicitly. To be explicit about all content types, set this to `'self'`. This ensures that, by default, content can only come from the originating host.

- `connect-src`: This applies to WebSockets, XHR/AJAX, and `EventSource`.
- `font-src`: This indicates sources you trust to deliver fonts.
- `frame-src`: This indicates which sources you want to permit in any `iframe` elements.
- `img-src`: This indicates which hosts can serve your app images.
- `media-src`: This indicates sources that can deliver audio and video content.
- `object-src`: This indicates sources that can deliver other object-based content (such as Flash).
- `style-src`: This indicates which origins are acceptable for CSS.
- `script-src`: This indicates which origins can serve JavaScript.

Although tempting to set the header to `default-src 'self'` and leave it at that, don't forget that your mobile app will be running locally and content will need to come from your server and not just from the actual origin (`file:///`). In addition, some platforms use an embedded `iframe` to communicate between the web and native portions of Cordova. The following example shows how to support Cordova apps while also allowing remote content via SSL and secure WebSocket from a server we trust:

```
<meta http-equiv="Content-Security-Policy"
content="default-src 'self' https://pge-as.example.com:4443
wss://pge-as.example.com:5999 gap://*"/>
```

For more information about this header, see `https://developer.mozilla.org/en-US/docs/Web/Security/CSP/CSP_policy_directives`. For browser support (which is quite good), see `http://caniuse.com/contentsecuritypolicy`.

Avoiding JSONP

JSONP is tempting because it gets around the same-origin restrictions that browsers enforce for web content. You should avoid it whenever possible because the browser is executing data as code in order to process the JSONP. This creates a huge security hole. Instead, where the same-origin policy applies, you should use **Cross-Origin Resource Sharing (CORS)**.

Unfortunately, you need access to the backend in order to enable CORS. This is fine for servers we own; however, if you're accessing third-party data, the third party is the only one who can enable CORS for you.

The HTTP header is as follows:

```
Access-Control-Allow-Origin: origin list
```

Specifying an asterisk as a wildcard will permit all origins to request the data. If using credentials, `Access-Control-Allow-Credentials` must also be `true`, but this doesn't work if you use a wildcard. Instead, you can return the request's origin for the same effect.

For more information regarding CORS, see `http://www.html5rocks.com/en/tutorials/cors/`. For browser support (which is quite good), see `http://caniuse.com/cors`.

Avoiding the use of iframes

As tempting as it might be to frame in some content from another source, it's best that you don't. If you absolutely must, be sure to use the `sandbox` attribute so that you limit the potential damage:

```
<iframe src="https://www.google.com" sandbox />
```

This is probably too restrictive for most sites, so you'll have to relax the sandbox based on the site you want to load. For more information on how to do this, see `http://www.html5rocks.com/en/tutorials/security/sandboxed-iframes/`.

Using TLS/SSL always

Although it seems incredibly obvious, there have been more than a few occasions where, either by accident or ignorance, sensitive traffic is sent over the wire in the clear. This is particularly dangerous when the information includes personally identifiable information, credit card and other financial information, health information, and other very sensitive data. Even for less sensitive data, it's still wise to avoid sending data in the clear, as it is incredibly easy to corrupt or inject it with malicious data.

Authentication

Authentication is scary, and rightly so, it is the gateway by which your users access critical data that needs to be protected, and it is critical that authentication be handled with care.

The following are some of my thoughts on how you should handle authentication in your apps:

- Avoid building your own authentication system. A well-tested and verified third-party authentication system is almost always better than anything you can build on your own. Make the third-party agent or software responsible to manage usernames and passwords and the security around all of that. Some examples are LDAP, Kerberos, OAuth, OpenID and Active Directory.

- Even though your client says that it has successfully authenticated doesn't mean that it has. Never trust your client. Ensure that the client has the proper authentication protocols in place rather than your backend code relying on a simple *I'm authenticated, honest!* flag.

- Never store the username and password *anywhere*. Of course, your code must check with the server if the username and password are valid, but the username and password should be forgotten once you send the request to the server. This is not completely foolproof, but you can reduce the attack surface if this information helps.

- Use tokens, if possible, to verify authentication after the initial request. Tokens should be treated as if they are the username and password because they grant the same kind of access. This means that tokens should not be stored as plain text. Most token-based systems have a huge benefit, however, tokens can easily be revoked. This means that should the provider be compromised, they can revoke all the tokens in one fell swoop after noticing the problem (and all the user needs to do is log back in with their credentials). Users themselves can often revoke their token as well. OAuth is a commonly used token-based system.

- Don't store authentication data in the clear (as plain text) *anywhere*. You cannot be assured of the integrity of your user's device (which might be jail broken, rooted, or otherwise compromised), nor can the integrity of your own servers be guaranteed. It is better if your attacker uses brute-force to compromise your data rather than leave the data out in the open, where an attacker can easily access it without being noticed.

- Don't encrypt passwords, *hash* them instead (and use salts). Encryption can always be reverse engineered; hashes need to be brute-forced. Always make sure that the hash space is large enough to ensure that every password generates a unique hash, otherwise it is possible to craft a fake password that still grants access by hashing to the same value as a legitimate password.

- Don't use **MDA5**, SHA1, and so on. These are designed to be fast algorithms intended to hash large amounts of data quickly. This also means that they can be brute-forced quickly. Use bcrypt, scrypt, pbkdf2, and so on.

- Use **cryptographic nonces**. A cryptographic nonce is a number used once and only once. It can be used to ensure that actions within a system can't simply be replayed since actions with an invalid nonce are discarded. The nonce is often random or pseudo-random (and the more truly random the better).

- If you must store authentication data, store them in secure, encrypted containers. On iOS, for example, one can store this information in a keychain. Keep in mind, of course, that if the keychain is on the user's device, it can be easily compromised. This is again why having a token instead of a username/password combination is so important because the token can be revoked.

- Balance the needs of the user, to have unfettered access to your system without continual need for re-authentication. This is essential to protect your data. Many systems will time a session out if no activity is seen within a given period of time. Invariably, users complain that they are *timed-out* too often. Other systems won't ask for authentication for several days or weeks, but if the user enables such an option on a shared or compromised computer, it is at the risk of an easy attack vector.

- Carefully balance the needs between extremely complex password requirements and the needs of your users. An extremely complex password with lots of numbers and symbols is likely to be written down, whereas a simpler password is easier for the user to remember. An easy way to create secure passwords is to use passphrases rather than passwords. For example, `HorseDoppler3$PumpkinQuilt` is easy to remember while being secure (you probably already have it memorized), whereas `H0$4iujmw23@r32z` is secure, but difficult to recall.

- Offer feedback to your users when asking them to set a password. Users are more likely to use secure passwords if they have an idea of how much more they need to do in order to create a secure password. Make the user work for a *good* rating; if your feedback indicates a password is secure too soon, your users will invariably use insecure passwords.

- Change passwords frequently. The longer a password is active, the more likely it is to be cracked. You do need to balance this with the pushback from your users: users do *not* like changing their passwords. Aim for changing passwords around every three to six months.

- Ensure that no account can be brute-forced without being quickly locked. Users are mistake-prone, so weigh carefully how many failed attempts should constitute a locked account. Consider locking accounts after five or ten failed attempts.

If you're using Node.js, consider utilizing **Passport** (`http://passportjs.org`) in order to implement your server-side authentication. It can handle many different authentication strategies (as Passport calls them) that includes local hash-based authentication, OpenID Connect, OAuth 2.0, SAML 2.0, and more (though you'll need to download appropriate modules to add support).

Server-specific security precautions

Because very few apps are silos, we need to ensure that the backend is also secure using security best practices.

Securing your backend

It goes without saying that if your backend servers are vulnerable, your entire system is also vulnerable. This includes your app, the data it processes, and your infrastructure (one vulnerable server can often serve as a foothold for an invading attacker).

Although we can't cover every scenario, we can give a few guidelines:

- Prevent `root` from logging in directly; require `sudo` from specific accounts in order to perform tasks requiring administrative privileges.

- Create accounts for your specific applications and grant them only the rights they actually need to have (avoid programs running on your server as `root`).

- Configure **SSH** to permit authentication only via key. Not only is it nice to log in from a trusted machine without a password, it can also enhance security by preventing password authentication (passwords are shorter than typical key lengths, and so easier to crack). Be sure to utilize a strong passphrase on any keychains used to authenticate in this manner should the machine be lost. (You should, of course, remove the keys from your servers such an event.).

- If using password authentication, ensure that the password is strong, and change it on a regular basis. Ensure that the account is locked after too many failed attempts.

- Configure SSH to only allow specific users to log in (whitelist allowed accounts).

- Ensure your servers have a properly configured firewall.

- Ensure your database server has no access from the outside.

- Ensure your web server exposes the bare minimum number of ports necessary.

- Use nonstandard ports for services (such as 58241 instead of 22 for SSH).

- Tunnel connections over SSH, or else use a VPN.

- Tunnel database connections over SSH, even on internal networks, (unless your database has built-in encryption).

When developing the example app for this book, I found it useful to utilize Virtual Private Servers by DigitalOcean (`http://www.digitalocean.com`). You can have a new server provisioned in roughly a minute, and it ensures that you can model a real-life network topology without risking your development machine or installing local virtual servers and then installing the operating system, and so on. Of course, these don't exactly duplicate what a corporation might have in their server room, but it's sufficient for our purpose.

While it might seem like overkill to set up a couple of VPSs, it's incredibly useful. For one, it's immediately apparent if there's any connectivity issue between our mobile device and the servers, and if it works, we know it will work in the real world as well. If we had everything running on `localhost` and within the same network, it will be difficult to prove that the app will work in a real-life situation.

Our server layout looks something like the following figure:

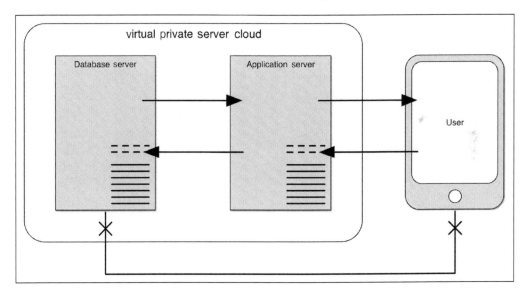

In the preceding layout, the database server has no direct contact with the user or the outside world. The database server does, however, implicitly trust the application server (but only if it is coming from within the internal network, not from without). This means we can access the database server via the application server, assuming we forward the appropriate ports. The application server, in turn, only exposes a port for SSH and HTTP. In the real world, we'd also have a gateway or firewall between the application server and the user. For additional security, the database server can only accept communication from the application server over certain ports as well.

If you want to know the specific steps I took to set up my VPSs so that they were reasonably secure (enough for a demonstration app, anyway), these steps are documented in the code package (`/digital-ocean/pge-db.md` and `/digital-ocean/pge-as.md`).

Hardening your backend against attack

Unfortunately, backends often implicitly trust their clients to a fault, especially their mobile clients, it is critical to verify and validate any data sent from a client in order to ensure that nothing untoward is going on.

Avoiding SQL injection

Never build SQL strings using any untrusted data. For example, never do the following:

```
var sql = "SELECT * FROM USERS WHERE USER_NAME='" + username + "'"
```

Should an attacker submit a username of `'John Smith'; DELETE FROM USERS; SELECT * FROM ANOTHER_TABLE WHERE FIELD=...`, then you've just literally lost all your user information, and the attacker gains access to a lot of other information as well.

Instead, use bind variables. The method depends largely upon the database driver library you use, but the following is an example:

```
connection.execute ("SELECT * FROM USERS WHERE USER_NAME=?",
[username]);
```

Preventing cross-site request forgeries

Otherwise known as a **replay attack**, an attacker could resend requests to your server potentially loaded with malicious content. There's only one good way to avoid this: require something that changes in every request to ensure its validity. The easiest way to do this is to have the client request a cryptographically random token from your server prior to performing requests that might change or delete data. Therefore, when the request is actually sent to change or delete data, the server checks that the token the client sent matches the one the server gave out before. If the tokens match, the request is carried out. If the token doesn't match, the request is denied.

How you accomplish this will vary based on the technologies your backend uses, but for Node.js and Express 4, it's as simple as including the `csurf`, `express-session`, and `cookie-parser` modules plus a little bit of code (see the *Quick Node.js/Express Server Security Settings* section later in this chapter).

Avoid trusting your client's state

Essentially, this means that you should *never* assume that your client's state is that of your backend. It's tempting, for example, to assume that your client will never ask for data that it doesn't have access to. If you code your backend with this assumption, an attacker can modify your client code or impersonate your client and request information to which they shouldn't have access; thus defeating any security you might have placed in the client.

Or in other words, apply your application's security at every tier, the database tier, the application server tier, *and* the mobile tier.

Verify message integrity with HMACs

This most often comes up when calling APIs; you need to ensure that no one has tampered with the message itself, but how can you be sure?

The easiest method is to sign the message with a hash, a shared secret, and a timestamp. The latter is present to ensure that the same message won't generate the same hash twice (otherwise it can be part of a replay attack), and the secret ensures that an attacker can't craft a valid hash of a malicious message without knowing the secret.

It's not a perfect guarantor of your message's authenticity, but it's one defense that's pretty easy to implement. Keep in mind, however, that should you decide to implement hashing routines on the client you must also keep the secret out of your JavaScript code. Otherwise the secret would be humanly-readable. Instead, it will be better for your client code to request a shared secret that can be used.

Most HMACs are also time sensitive. This does cause a potential issue if your client and server are not within a few seconds or minutes of each other. Most mobile devices ensure that their clocks are kept current, but you'll also want to ensure your servers synchronize their time from an NTP server.

Furthermore, you can mitigate this issue to a small degree by calculating HMACs for timestamps a few minutes prior and few minutes after the current time on the server. This allows the client's time to vary by a small degree. For example, if a timestamp only contained the date and time accurate to the minute, the client's time can vary by several seconds. Most servers will go one step further and allow several minutes on either side of the current time. Our demonstration app does just this; a timestamp can be as much as five minutes fast or slow and the message will still be accepted.

Quick Node.js and Express server security settings

If you're using Node.js with Express, you only need a small amount of code and an additional module to help with your security.

First, install `helmet`, `express-session`, `cookie-parser`, and `csurf`:

```
npm install helmet --save
npm install express-session --save
npm install cookie-parser --save
npm install csurf --save
```

Then use the following middleware commands:

```
var express = require('express');
var helmet = require('helmet');
var cookieParser = require('cookie-parser');
var session = require('express-session');
var csrf = require('csurf');
var app=express();
// showing what our server is powered by just makes the attacker's
// job that much easier, so disable it
app.disable ( "x-powered-by" );
// security enhancements via helmet
app.use(helmet.csp({
    defaultSrc: ["'self'", "pge-as.example.com"],
    safari5: false  // safari5 has buggy behavior
}));
app.use(helmet.xframe()); // no framing our content!
```

```
app.use(helmet.xssFilter()); // old IE won't get this, since some
// implementations are buggy
app.use(helmet.hsts({maxAge: 15552000, includeSubDomains: true}));
// force SSL for six months
app.use(helmet.ienoopen()); // keep IE from executing downloads
app.use(helmet.nosniff()); // keep IE from sniffing mime types
app.use(cookieParser());
app.use(session( {
    secret: "a secret",
    key: "sessionId",
    cookie: { httpOnly: true, secure: true},
    resave: true,
    saveUninitialized: true
}));
// cors setup
var corsDelegate = function ( req, cb ) {
    var corsOptions = { origin: true, credentials: true };
    cb( null, corsOptions );
};
app.use( cors( corsDelegate ) );
// Make sure CORS is there for preflight OPTIONS requests
app.options( "*", cors( corsDelegate ) ); // csrf security
app.use(csrf());
app.use(function (req, res, next) {
    res.locals.csrftoken = req.csrfToken();
    next();
});
```

Don't forget to use SSL:

```
var fs = require('fs');
var SSLOptions = {
    key: fs.readFileSync ('_certs/tasker1.key'),
    cert: fs.readFileSync ('_certs/tasker1.cer'),
    ca: fs.readFileSync ('_certs/ssca.cer')
};
app.set('port', config.get('express:port') );
var server = https.createServer (SSLOptions, app).listen(app.
get('port'), function() {
});
```

Cordova-specific security precautions

Now that we've covered general and server security, let's deal with some security issues that are specific to mobile devices and Cordova apps.

Targeting modern mobile devices

Although your marketing department will cringe to hear me say this, targeting only modern devices is extremely important in order to maintain security. Older mobile devices (such as Android 2.x or lower) have several security vulnerabilities that will never be patched. In short, avoid them completely even if they still form a big part of the market.

I would highly suggest avoiding any device running a version of Android less than 4.x version. Cordova doesn't support Android version 3.x (Honeycomb), and version 2.x has too many issues to be secure. iOS users, on the other hand, often get security updates for their devices for two years and sometimes longer. Even so, I wouldn't support devices running iOS 5 or lower.

Source code protection

At this point, we're going to switch gears from the backend and focus for a moment on the frontend.

 There's something very important that you need to know about Cordova apps: your HTML, CSS, and JavaScript is visible to anyone who can download your app.

Native code is a compiled representation of a program. This means that the code is inherently obfuscated, and it isn't immediately obvious what the code does simply by looking at it. It's a little harder to find implementation details that might open an app up to attack (though this is by no means impossible).

Non-native code such as HTML, CSS, and JavaScript is not compiled at all. This means that your implementation details are easily accessible to anyone who understands the technology at even a fairly basic level, including any sensitive implementation details. This should immediately raise some red flags in your mind such as:

- Encryption keys, sensitive data, and so on should never be stored within your code

- Your backend should never implicitly trust your frontend

None of this should be news, it's just that the way Cordova apps are packaged and installed means it is *that* much more important you are aware of the inherent security risks. (And don't forget that your intellectual property is also on full display, which means it is easier for a competitor to see how you implemented a particular feature.)

Most users aren't going to pry into your code and modify it. We aren't terribly concerned with those users; it's the malicious user or other attacker that keep us awake at night. The following are a few scenarios to worry about:

- John Doe is a disgruntled employee with a technical background. He downloads the app and installs it on his mobile device. He then connects his mobile device to his computer and installs a program that allows him to browse the filesystem from his mobile device. He finds your HTML, CSS, and JavaScript. He downloads the files and creates a new version of your app designed to send malicious commands to your application server. Should your application server and database server implicitly trust the client, John Doe can successfully wipe out your system, causing a huge headache. (Hopefully there's a good backup around!)

- Jane Smith is intent on maliciously attacking your system. She downloads your app to her computer and extracts its contents. She finds various security holes simply by looking at your code, and this gives her everything she needs to know to gain access and leak your important data to the outside world.

- Gerald Scott wants to make some quick money on the app store. He downloads your app onto his computer, changes some assets, repackages the changes with Cordova, and publishes it back to the app store. Perhaps he even makes a few malicious changes so that he gets a copy of any username and password submitted to the app by the user. He renames the app on the store to something close to (but not quite) the original name, and manages to fool several users into installing it. To the best of their knowledge, nothing is wrong, but Gerald can now be in control of several passwords.

Although all the preceding sounds dire, it is important to remember that this isn't unique to Cordova. Native apps are subject to the very same attacks, but it is usually a little harder to accomplish. Of course, for a suitably determined attacker, nothing is invulnerable; it just takes more time and effort.

Most developers will immediately wonder if there is a good way around their code being so visible. If you want to defeat the casual user who is just browsing around to see what they can find, minifying your JavaScript will probably suffice (minifying usually has a good deal of obfuscation as a side effect). However, minified JavaScript code can be reconstructed; therefore, this is no obstacle for the attacker with a little more patience.

The next thought is to encrypt the code. Technically you can do this, but you have a problem: where do you store the encryption key? If you put it in your native code, a slightly more determined attacker can locate the key and undo your encryption. In fact, if this key resides *anywhere on the device*, your code can be compromised.

So what is a security-conscious developer supposed to do? My advice is simple: minify your code if you wish, but don't bother encrypting it. Avoid putting encryption keys, or secrets, or other sensitive information into your code in the first place.

For the absolutely determined, there's one more method: download all your code from the server (or only the most sensitive portions). This one is on shaky ground—it may not pass review in some app stores (though if you are deploying internally, that's not an issue)—and it only throws up an additional obstacle. A really determined individual with a suitably hacked device can easily pull whatever code you send from your server from the mobile device's memory.

In other words, you can't protect your code, native or otherwise. You can only make it more difficult for an attacker to compromise. The question ultimately becomes this: *when does adding more and more layers of protection in the code stop being cost-effective?* This is a question your enterprise can answer.

Using InAppBrowser for external links

Because your Cordova app is actually a browser running JavaScript, CSS, and HTML, it's also possible to link to external content directly in the same browser. This is dangerous because it grants the external resource access to the native bridge.

Instead, use the InAppBrowser plugin to load these external pages; this doesn't have access to the native bridge at all. You can add the plugin by using the following code line:

```
cordova plugin add org.apache.cordova.inappbrowser
```

Any link with a `target` of `_blank` will open in InAppBrowser, or you can use `window.open` as follows:

```
var ref = window.open("http://www.cnn.com", "_blank", "location=yes");
```

It should also be noted that the same security risk applies to any `iframe` displayed within your app. InAppBrowser won't help you here, so it's better to avoid using `iframes` with untrusted content.

Whitelisting domains

When running your Cordova app on a user's device, you might want to ensure that the app can only talk to your server. This can reduce your risks of an XSS attack.

You can whitelist your server in the Cordova app's `config.xml` file as follows:

```
<access origin="https://pge-as.example.com" />
```

If you need to broaden access to any subdomain, you can use this:

```
<access origin="https://*.example.com" />
```

Be absolutely certain to remove any access rules you don't need, and be aware that Cordova apps ship with a rule that allows access to any server by default.

For more information, visit `http://cordova.apache.org/docs/en/edge/guide_appdev_whitelist_index.md.html#Whitelist%20Guide`.

Avoiding self-signed certificates

Although incredibly tempting for various reasons (least of which is cost and ease in generating a certificate), it's best to avoid self-signed certificates if you can. There are lots of reasons as to why it is better to use a certificate signed by a well-trusted **certificate authority** (**CA**), but when dealing with Cordova, one reason in particular stands out more often than not: when someone has a communication problem with the backend, it nearly always boils down to a self-signed certificate. Because there's no mechanism to trust the self-signed certificate, Cordova tends to reject the certificate outright.

If you *must* use self-signed certificates, you should perform the following steps (from `http://blog.httpwatch.com/2013/12/12/five-tips-for-using-self-signed-ssl-certificates-with-ios/`):

1. Create your own certificate authority and root CA certificate as follows:

   ```
   openssl genrsa -out ssca.key 2048
   openssl req -x509 -new -key ssca.key -out ssca.cer -days
   730 -subj /CN="Example Corporation CA"
   ```

2. Install `ssca.cer` on your devices (you can e-mail them to the device, or you can use the platform's management software to push a profile containing the certificate to your users).

3. Create your self-signed certificate(s) as follows:

```
openssl genrsa -out tasker1.key 2048
openssl req -new -out tasker1.req -key tasker1.key -subj /CN=pge-
as.example.com
openssl x509 -req -in tasker1.req -out tasker1.cer -CAkey ssca.key
-CA ssca.cer -days 365 -CAcreateserial -CAserial serial
```

4. Install your self-signed certificates on your user's mobile devices (for example, on iOS, you can send a certificate via e-mail and install it, or install it using Apple's iPhone Configuration utility).

Although this works on iOS (send the cert via e-mail and open the certificate attachment or utilize Apple's iPhone Configuration utility) and Android (use `adb push ssca.cer /sdcard/`, and navigate to **Settings** | **Personal** | **Security** | **Credential Storage** | **Install from storage**), you will want to verify that there is a mechanism available to install certificates on any other platform you intend to use.

Using a well-known certificate authority

It's not possible, unfortunately, for mobile platforms to ship with root CA certificates for every certificate authority around, so you should consult with a specific CA prior to purchasing a certificate to ensure that their certificate will work properly on your targeted mobile devices. Some well-known CAs are as follows:

- StartSSL (`http://www.startssl.com`, free certificate available)
- Comodo Positive SSL (`http://www.positivessl.com`, 30-day free trial)
- DigiCert (`http://www.digicert.com`)
- SSL.com (`http://www.ssl.com`, 90-day free trial)
- Entrust (`http://www.entrust.net`)
- Symantec (`http://www.symantec.com/verisign/ssl-certificates`, 30-day free trial)

Man-in-the-middle attacks

When we're developing apps that require communication between the user and our servers, we tend to have a skewed idea of how this actually works. We tend to maintain a pretty simple model of the interaction in our heads, something like the following figure:

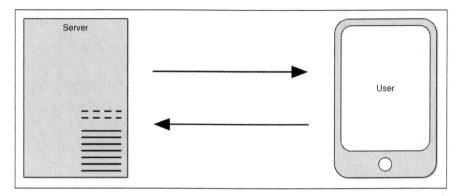

Of course, this is rarely ever the case (except possibly in development). More likely, the model is something more like the following figure:

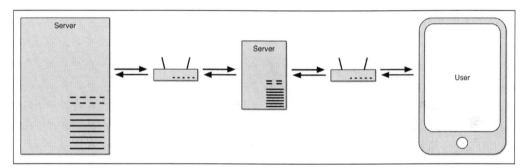

When dealing with communication over the Internet, there are a lot of routers and servers that get to see the data flowing between the user and your internal systems — and this is why it is so critical that you always use TLS/SSL or a VPN — otherwise your data is clearly visible to all of these systems.

However, even if one uses TLS/SSL, it doesn't mean that one isn't vulnerable to what is called a **man-in-the-middle** attack. What happens in this kind of attack is that an attacker inserts themselves into the communication loop between the user and the server as shown in the following figure:

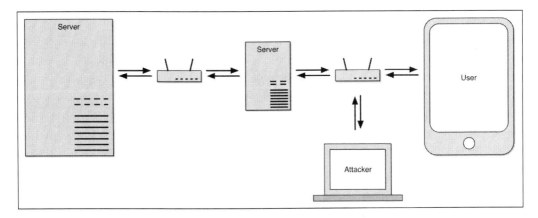

One major common attack vector is via unsecured Wi-Fi networks. Once the unsuspecting user connects to an infected network, the attacker can intercept, modify, and resend any traffic they see fit. Although it's easiest with non-encrypted traffic, it's also possible to spoof an SSL certificate, and it is unlikely the user would notice that something was terribly wrong.

There is a simple way to ensure if there is a *man-in-the-middle* attack in your communication stream. It's called **certificate pinning**.

The idea is really quite simple: as a developer, we know exactly what certificate is being used on the server. Therefore, we can check on the client if it received that exact certificate. For example, if we can compare the certificate's fingerprint with our client code, we can verify if the certificate we received is the same certificate we expected.

You might note that this is inherently insecure if an attacker has access to the code running on our device as it will be easy to disable the certificate check. What we're doing is increasing the attack surface by adding additional obstacles that will have to be compromised in order for an attack to succeed. In other words, the man in the middle will also need to have successfully attacked the mobile device *and* removed the certificate check as well. Although not impossible, it's increasingly unlikely.

Cordova doesn't offer certificate pinning, but there is a third-party plugin that offers fingerprint checking (which comes close). Although not perfect, it's far better than nothing, and can be used to give a high level of confidence that the data transmission between backend and frontend is indeed secure. The plugin is available at `https://github.com/EddyVerbruggen/SSLCertificateChecker-PhoneGap-Plugin`.

Using this plugin is pretty simple. It can be installed by running the following:

```
cordova plugin add
https://github.com/EddyVerbruggen/SSLCertificateChecker-PhoneGap-
Plugin.git
```

In your JavaScript code, authenticity can then be verified by doing this:

```
window.plugins.sslCertificateChecker.check ( successHandler,
failureHandler, "https://pge-as.example.com",
    "27 02 A5 EB 95 91 41 66 C3 9F 82 D3 59 14 13 0E 13 B5 13
9E");
function successHandler (message) {
 // message is CONNECTION_SECURE
}
function failureHandler (message) {
 // message is either CONNECTION_NOT_SECURE or CONNECTION_FAILED
}
```

Because Cordova doesn't offer true certificate pinning, it is all the more important that you use a certificate signed by a well-known certificate authority.

Local data store security/encryption

Unfortunately, there aren't many good solutions to ensure the integrity of locally stored data, which is why you should avoid storing any sensitive data to the user's device.

Most importantly, avoid storing sensitive data using `localStorage` or web storage. These are often backed by a simple SQLite database that is not encrypted. Anyone who has access to the device and can unlock it can browse the data in clear text. `sessionStorage` is a little safer since it will be removed when the app is closed, but still should not be used for sensitive data such as authorization tokens or passwords.

iOS has the concept of a keychain. This keychain is designed to store sensitive information. None of this is completely secure, of course, since it still resides in the user's device and there are known attacks against the keychain. Even so, it's better than any other storage location on iOS. In Android, data written to internal storage is intended to be private to your app, but this doesn't necessarily hold true if the device is rooted or otherwise compromised.

The iOS keychain plugin for Cordova is available at `http://plugins.cordova.io/#/package/com.shazron.cordova.plugin.keychainutil`

To store anything more complex than key/value data, you'll almost certainly need to use a database. For most platforms, SQLite is really the only choice, though you shouldn't attempt to use the browser's implementation (otherwise called web storage). Instead, use a third-party plugin such as: `https://github.com/brodysoft/Cordova-SQLitePlugin`.

SQLite also supports encryption via SQLCipher (`http://sqlcipher.net`), but you need to be careful to avoid storing the encryption secret in your JavaScript code. If you obtain your secret from the server or use some other data, it becomes a good choice for sensitive data.

Of course, most modern mobile devices support some level of encryption when the device is locked. This is not guaranteed to prevent attacks, and mobile operating systems are always being patched to catch up to these new attacks. So don't rely on the mobile device's encryption to protect plain-text data you store on the device as it can and will probably be compromised at some point.

Summary

We covered a lot in this chapter. Most of the security practices are practices that can be applied to any number of situations. We also covered security issues that are specific to Cordova and mobile apps.

If anything, it should be clear now that writing secure mobile apps that communicate with your enterprise servers is anything but simple. This chapter can help serve as a reference for common security issues and fixes, but you might also want to look at the section entitled *Security Resources* in *Appendix, Useful Resources*.

In the next chapter, we'll start building our middle tier and the API that supports our sample app.

4
Building the Middle-Tier

If you browse any Cordova/PhoneGap forum, you'll often come across posts asking how to connect to and query a backend database. In this chapter, we will look at the reasons why it is necessary to interact with your backend database using an intermediary service. If the business logic resides within the database, the middle-tier might be a very simple layer wrapping the data store, but it can also implement a significant portion of business logic as well. The middle-tier also usually handles session authentication logic.

Although many enterprise projects will already have a middle-tier in place, it's useful to understand how a middle-tier works, and how to implement one if you ever need to build a solution from the ground up.

In this chapter, we'll focus heavily on these topics:

- Typical middle-tier architecture
- Designing a RESTful-like API
- Implementing a RESTful-like hypermedia API using Node.js
- Connecting to the backend database
- Executing queries
- Handling authentication using **Passport**
- Building API handlers

 You are welcome to implement your middle-tier using any technology with which you are comfortable. The topics that we will cover in this chapter can be applied to any middle-tier platform.

Middle-tier architecture

It's tempting, especially for simple applications, to have the desire to connect your mobile app directly to your data store. This is an incredibly bad idea, which means your data store is vulnerable and exposed to attacks from the outside world (unless you require the user to log in to a VPN). It also means that your mobile app has a lot of code dedicated solely to querying your data store, which makes for a tightly coupled environment. If you ever want to change your database platform or modify the table structures, you will need to update the app, and any app that wasn't updated will stop working. Furthermore, if you want another system to access the data, for example, a reporting solution, you will need to repeat the same queries and logic already implemented in your app in order to ensure consistency.

For these reasons alone, it's a bad idea to directly connect your mobile app to your backend database. However, there's one more good reason: Cordova has no nonlocal database drivers *whatsoever*.

Although it's not unusual for a desktop application to make a direct connection to your database on an internal network, Cordova has no facility to load a database driver to interface directly with an Oracle or MySQL database. This means that you *must* build an intermediary service to bridge the gap from your database backend to your mobile app.

No middle-tier is exactly the same, but for web and mobile apps, this intermediary service — also called an application server — is typically a relatively simple web server. This server accepts incoming requests from a client (our mobile app or a website), processes them, and returns the appropriate results. In order to do so, the web server parses these requests using a variety of middleware (security, session handling, cookie handling, request parsing, and so on) and then executes the appropriate request handler for the request. This handler then needs to pass this request on to the business logic handler, which, in our case, lives on the database server. The business logic will determine how to react to the request and returns the appropriate data to the request handler. The request handler transforms this data into something usable by the client, for example, JSON or XML, and returns it to the client.

The middle-tier provides an **Application Programming Interface (API)**. Beyond authentication and session handling, the middle-tier provides a set of reusable components that perform specific tasks by delegating these tasks to lower tiers. As an example, one of the components of our Tasker app is named `get-task-comments`. Provided the user is properly authenticated, the component will request a specific task from the business logic and return the attached comments. Our mobile app (or any other consumer) only needs to know how to call `get-task-comments`. This decouples the client from the database and ensures that we aren't unnecessarily repeating code.

The flow of request and response looks a lot like the following figure:

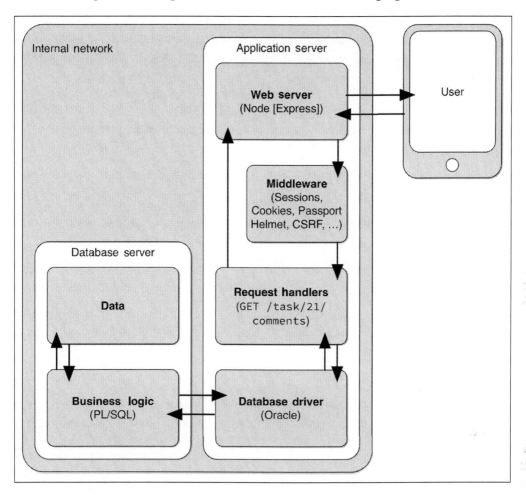

Designing a RESTful-like API

A mobile app interfaces with your business logic and data store via an API provided by the application server middle-tier. Exactly how this API is implemented and how the client uses it is up to the developers of the system. In the past, this has often meant using web services (over HTTP) with information interchange via **Simple Object Access Protocol (SOAP)**.

Recently, RESTful APIs have become the norm when working with web and mobile applications. These APIs conform to the following constraints:

- **Client/Server**: Clients are not concerned with how data is stored, (that's the server's job), and servers are not concerned with state (that's the client's job). They should be able to be developed and/or replaced completely independently of each other (low coupling) as long as the API remains the same.

- **Stateless**: Each request should have the necessary information contained within it so that the server can properly handle the request. The server isn't concerned about session states; this is the sole domain of the client.

- **Cacheable**: Responses must specify if they can be cached or not. Proper management of this can greatly improve performance and scalability.

- **Layered**: The client shouldn't be able to tell if there are any intermediary servers between it and the server. This ensures that additional servers can be inserted into the chain to provide caching, security, load balancing, and so on.

- **Code-on-demand**: This is an optional constraint. The server can send the necessary code to handle the response to the client. For a mobile PhoneGap app, this might involve sending a small snippet of JavaScript, for example, to handle how to display and interact with a Facebook post.

- **Uniform Interface**: Resources are identified by a **Uniform Resource Identifier (URI)**, for example, `https://pge-as.example.com/task/21` refers to the task with an identifier of 21. These resources can be expressed in any number of formats to facilitate data interchange. Furthermore, when the client has the resource (in whatever representation it is provided), the client should also have enough information to manipulate the resource. Finally, the representation should indicate valid state transitions by providing links that the client can use to navigate the **state tree** of the system.

There are many good web APIs in production, but often they fail to address the last constraint very well. They might represent resources using URIs, but typically the client is expected to know all the endpoints of the API and how to transition between them without the server telling the client how to do so. This means that the client is tightly coupled to the API. If the URIs or the API change, then the client breaks.

RESTful APIs should instead provide all the valid state transitions with each response. This lets the client reduce its coupling by looking for specific actions rather than assuming that a specific URI request will work. Properly implemented, the underlying URIs could change and the client app would be unaffected. The only thing that needs to be constant is the entry URI to the API.

There are many good examples of these kinds of APIs, PayPal's is quite good as are many others. The responses from these APIs always contain enough information for the client to advance to the next state in the chain. So in the case of PayPal, a response will always contain enough information to advance to the next step of the monetary transaction. Because the response contains this information, the client only needs to look at the response rather than having the URI of the next step hardcoded. For more good examples, see the *RESTful-like API Resources* section in *Appendix, Useful Resources*.

RESTful APIs aren't standardized; one API might provide links to the next state in one format, while another API might use a different format. That said, there are several attempts to create a standard response format, Collection+JSON is just one example. The lack of standardization in the response format isn't as bad as it sounds; the more important issue is that as long as your app understands the response format, it can be decoupled from the URI structure of your API and its resources. The API becomes a list of methods with explicit transitions rather than a list of URIs alone. As long as the action names remain the same, the underlying URIs can be changed without affecting the client.

This works well when it comes to most APIs where authorization is provided using an API key or an encoded token. For example, an API will often require authorization via OAuth 2.0. Your code asks for the proper authorization first, and upon each subsequent request, it passes an appropriate token that enables access to the requested resource.

Where things become problematic, *and* why we're calling our API *RESTful-like,* is when it comes to the end user authentication. Whether the user of our mobile app recognizes it or not, they are an immediate consumer of our API. Because the data itself is protected based upon the roles and access of each particular user, users must authenticate themselves prior to accessing any data.

When an end user is involved with authentication, the idea of sessions is inevitably required largely for the end user's convenience. Some sessions can be incredibly short-lived, for example, many banks will terminate a session if no activity is seen for 10 minutes, while others can be long-lived, and others might even be effectively eternal until explicitly revoked by the user. Regardless of the session length, the fact that a session is present indicates that the server must often store some information about state. Even if this information applies only to the user's authentication and session validity, it still violates the second rule of RESTful APIs.

Tasker's web API, then, is a RESTful-like API. In everything except session handling and authentication, our API is like any other RESTful API. However, when it comes to authentication, the server maintains some state in order to ensure that users are properly authenticated.

In the case of Tasker, the maintained state is limited. Once a user authenticates, a unique single-use token and an Hash Message Authentication Code (HMAC) secret are generated and returned to the client. This token is expected to be sent with the next API request and this request is expected to be signed with the HMAC secret. Upon completion of this API request, a new token is generated. Each token expires after a specified amount of time, or can be expired immediately by an explicit logout.

Each token is stored in the backend, which means we violate the stateless rule. Our tokens are just a cryptographically random series of bytes, and because of this, there's nothing in the token that can be used to identify the user. This means we need to maintain the valid tokens and their user associations in the database. If the token contained user-identifiable information, we could technically avoid maintaining state, but this also means that the token could be forged if the attacker knew how tokens were constructed. A random token, on the other hand, means that there's no method of construction that can fool the server; the attacker will have to be very lucky to guess it right. Since Tasker's tokens are continually expiring after a short period of time and are continually regenerated upon each request, guessing a token is that much more difficult. Of course, it's not impossible for an attacker to get lucky and guess the right token on the first try, but considering the amount of entropy in most usernames and passwords, it's more likely that the attacker could guess the user's password than they could guess the correct token.

Because these tokens are managed by the backend, our Tasker's API isn't truly stateless, and so it's not truly RESTful, hence the term RESTful-like. If you want to implement your API as a pure RESTful API, feel free. If your API is like that of many other APIs (such as Twitter, PayPal, Facebook, and so on), you'll probably want to do so.

All this sounds well and good, but how should we go about designing and defining our API? Here's how I suggest going about it:

1. Identify the resources. In Tasker, the resources are people, tasks, and task comments. Essentially, these are the data models. (If you take security into account, Tasker also has user and role resources in addition to sessions.)

2. Define how the URI should represent the resource. For example, Bob Smith might be represented by `/person/bob-smith` or `/person/29481`. Query parameters are also acceptable: `/person?administeredBy=john-doe` will refer to the set of all individuals who have John Doe as their administrator. If this helps, think of each instance of a resource and each collection of these resources as web pages each having their own URL.

3. Identify the actions that can be performed for each resource. For example, a task can be created and modified by the owner of the task. This task can be assigned to another user. A task's status and progress can be updated by both the owner and the assignee. With RESTful APIs, these actions are typically handled by using the HTTP verbs (also known as methods) GET, POST, PUT, and DELETE. Others can also be used, such as OPTIONS, PATCH, and so on. We'll cover in a moment how these usually line up against typical **Create, Read, Update, Delete (CRUD)** operations.

4. Identify the state transitions that are valid for resources. As an example, a client's first steps might be to request a list of all tasks assigned to a particular user. As part of the response, it should be given URIs that indicate how the app should retrieve information about a particular task. Furthermore, within this single task's response, there should be information that tells the client how to modify the task.

Most APIs generally mirror the typical CRUD operations. The following is how the HTTP verbs line up against the familiar CRUD counterparts for a collection of items:

HTTP verb	CRUD operation	Description
GET	READ	This returns the collection of items in the desired format. Often can be filtered and sorted via query parameters.
POST	CREATE	This creates an item within the collection. The return result includes the URI for the new resource.
DELETE	N/A	This is not typically used at the collection level, unless one wants to remove the entire collection.
PUT	N/A	This is not typically used at the collection level, though it can be used to update/replace each item in the collection.

The same verbs are used for items within a collection:

HTTP verb	CRUD operation	Description
GET	READ	This returns a specific item, given the ID.
POST	N/A	This is not typically used at the item level.
DELETE	DELETE	This deletes a specific item, given the ID.
PUT	UPDATE	This updates an existing item. Sometimes PATCH is used to update only specific properties of the item.

Here's an example of a state transition diagram for a portion of the Tasker API along with the corresponding HTTP verbs:

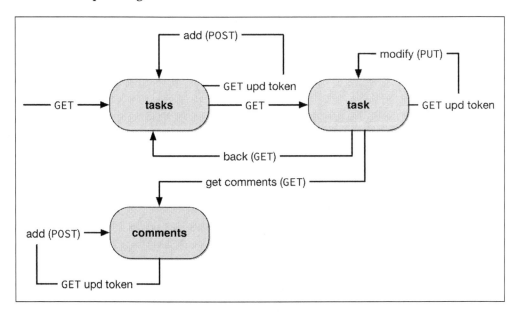

Now that we've determined the states and the valid transitions, we're ready to start modeling the API and the responses it should generate. This is particularly useful before you start coding, as one will often notice issues with the API during this phase, and it's far easier to fix them now rather than after a lot of code has been written (or worse, after the API is in production).

How you model your API is up to you. If you want to create a simple text document that describes the various requests and expected responses, that's fine. You can also use any number of tools that aid in modeling your API. Some even allow you to provide mock responses for testing. Some of these are identified as follows:

- **RAML** (http://raml.org): This is a markup language to model RESTful-like APIs. You can build API models using any text editor, but there is also an API designer online.

- **Apiary** (http://apiary.io): Apiary uses a markdown-like language (API blueprint) to model APIs. If you're familiar with markdown, you shouldn't have much trouble using this service. API mocking and automated testing are also provided.

- **Swagger** (http://swagger.io): This is similar to RAML, where it uses YAML as the modeling language. Documentation and client code can be generated directly from the API model.

Building our API using Node.js

In this section, we'll cover connecting our web service to our Oracle database, handling user authentication and session management using Passport, and defining handlers for state transitions.

You'll definitely want to take a look at the `/tasker-srv` directory in the code package for this book, which contains the full web server for Tasker. In the following sections, we've only highlighted some snippets of the code.

Connecting to the backend database

Node.js's community has provided a large number of database drivers, so chances are good that whatever your backend, Node.js has a driver available for it. In our example app, we're using an Oracle database as the backend, which means we'll be using the `oracle` driver (`https://www.npmjs.org/package/oracle`).

Connecting to the database is actually pretty easy, the following code shows how:

```
var oracle = require("oracle");
oracle.connect ( { hostname: "localhost", port: 1521,
   database: "xe",
user: "tasker", password: "password" },
function (err, client) {
   if (err) { /* error; return or next(err) */ }
   /* query the database; when done call client.close() */
});
```

Downloading the example code

You can download the example code files for all Packt books you have purchased from your account at `http://www.packtpub.com`. If you purchased this book elsewhere, you can visit `http://www.packtpub.com/support` and register to have the files e-mailed directly to you.

In the real world, a development version of our server will be using a test database, and a production version of our server will use the production database. To facilitate this, we made the connection information configurable. The `/config/development.json` and `/config/production.json` files contain connection information, and the main code simply requests the configuration information when making a connection, the following code line is used to get the configuration information:

```
oracle.connect ( config.get ( "oracle" ), … );
```

Since we're talking about the real world, we also need to recognize that database connections are slow and they need to be pooled in order to improve performance as well as permit parallel execution. To do this, we added the `generic-pool` NPM module (`https://www.npmjs.org/package/generic-pool`) and added the following code to `app.js`:

```
var clientPool = pool.Pool( {
  name: "oracle",
  create: function ( cb ) {
    return new oracle.connect( config.get("oracle"),
      function ( err, client ) {
        cb ( err, client );
      }
    )
  },
  destroy: function ( client ) {
    try {
      client.close();
    } catch (err) {
      // do nothing, but if we don't catch the error,
      // the server crashes
    }
  },
  max: 5,
  min: 1,
  idleTimeoutMillis: 30000
});
```

Because our pool will always contain at least one connection, we need to ensure that when the process exits, the pool is properly drained, as follows:

```
process.on("exit", function () {
  clientPool.drain( function () {
    clientPool.destroyAllNow();
  });
});
```

On its own, this doesn't do much yet. We need to ensure that the pool is available to the entire app:

```
app.set ( "client-pool", clientPool );
```

Executing queries

We've built our business logic in the Oracle database using PL/SQL stored procedures and functions. In PL/SQL, functions can return table-like structures. While this is similar in concept to a view, writing a function using PL/SQL provides us more flexibility.

As such, our queries won't actually be talking to the base tables, they'll be talking to functions that return results based on the user's authorization. This means that we don't need additional conditions in a WHERE clause to filter based on the user's authorization, which helps eliminate code duplication.

Regardless of the previous statement, executing queries and stored procedures is done using the same method, that is execute. Before we can execute anything, we need to first acquire a client connection from the pool.

To this end, we added a small set of database utility methods; you can see the code in the /db-utils directory. The query utility method is shown in the following code snippet:

```
DBUtils.prototype.query = function ( sql, bindParameters, cb ) {
  var self = this,
    clientPool = self._clientPool,
    deferred = Q.defer();
    clientPool.acquire( function ( err, client ) {
    if ( err ) {
    winston.error("Failed to acquire connection.");
      if ( cb ) {
        cb( new Error( err ) );
      else {
        deferred.reject( err );
      }
    }
    }
    try {
      client.execute( sql, bindParameters,
        function ( err, results ) {
          if ( err ) {
            clientPool.release( client );
            if ( cb ) {
            cb( new Error( err ) );
            } else {
              deferred.reject( err );
            }
          }
          clientPool.release( client );
```

```
        if ( cb ) {
          cb( err, results );
        } else {
          deferred.resolve( results );
        }
      } );
    }
    catch ( err2 ) {
    try {
      clientPool.release( client );
    }
    catch ( err3 ) {
      // can't do anything...
    }
    if ( cb ) {
      cb( err2 );
    } else { deferred.reject( err2 ); }
    }
  }
  } );
  if ( !cb ) {
    return deferred.promise;
  }
};
```

It's then possible to retrieve the results to an arbitrary query using the preceding method, as shown in the following code snippet:

```
dbUtil.query( "SELECT * FROM " +
"table(tasker.task_mgmt.get_task(:1,:2))",
[ taskId, req.user.userId ] )
.then( function ( results ) {
  // if no results, return 404 not found
  if ( results.length === 0 ) {
    return next( Errors.HTTP_NotFound() );
  }
  // create a new task with the database results
  // (will be in first row)
  req.task = new Task( results[ 0 ] );
  return next();
} )
.catch( function ( err ) {
  return next( new Error( err ) );
} )
.done();
```

The query used in the preceding code is an example of calling a stored function that returns a table structure. The results of the SELECT statement will depend on parameters (taskId and username), and get_task will decide what data can be returned based on the user's authorization.

Using Passport to handle authentication and sessions

Although we've implemented our own authentication protocol, it's better that we use one that has already been well vetted and is well understood as well as one that suits our particular needs. In our case, we needed the demo to stand on its own without a lot of additional services, and as such, we built our own protocol. Even so, we chose a well known cryptographic method (PBKDF2), and are using a large number of iterations and large key lengths.

In order to implement authentication easily in Node.js, you'll probably want to use Passport (https://www.npmjs.org/package/passport). It has a large community, and supports a large number of authentication schemes. If at all possible, try to use third-party authentication systems as often as possible (for example, LDAP, AD, Kerberos, and so on).

In our case, because our authentication method is custom, we chose to use the passport-req strategy (https://www.npmjs.org/package/passport-req). Since Tasker's authentication is token-based, we will use this to inspect a custom header that the client will use to pass us the authentication token.

The following is a simplified diagram of how Tasker's authentication process works:

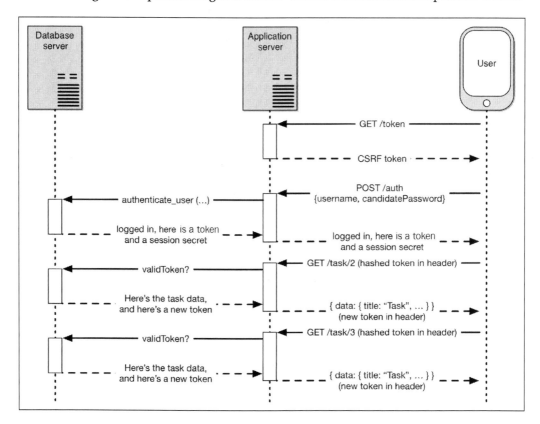

 Please don't use our authentication strategy for anything that requires high levels of security. It's just an example, and isn't guaranteed to be secure in any way.

Before we can actually use Passport, we need to define how our authentication strategy actually works. We do this by calling `passport.use` in our `app.js` file:

```
var passport = require("passport");
var ReqStrategy = require("passport-req").Strategy;
var Session = require("./models/session");
passport.use ( new ReqStrategy (
  function ( req, done ) {
    var clientAuthToken = req.headers["x-auth-token"];
    var session = new Session ( new DBUtils ( clientPool ) );
    session.findSession( clientAuthToken )
    .then( function ( results ) {
```

```
      if ( !results ) { return done( null, false ); }
      done( null, results );
      } )
      .catch( function ( err ) {
      return done( err );
      } )
      .done();
    }
) );
```

In the preceding code, we've given Passport a new authentication strategy. Now, whenever Passport needs to authenticate a request, it will call this small section of code. You might be wondering what's going on in findSession. Here's the code:

```
Session.prototype.findSession = function ( clientAuthToken, cb ) {
  var self = this,
  deferred = Q.defer();
  // if no token, no sense in continuing
  if ( typeof clientAuthToken === "undefined" ) {
    if ( cb ) { return cb( null, false ); }
    else { deferred.reject(); }
  }
  // an auth token is of the form 1234.ABCDEF10284128401ABC13...
  var clientAuthTokenParts = clientAuthToken.split( "." );
  if ( !clientAuthTokenParts ) {
    if ( cb ) { return cb( null, false ); }
    else { deferred.reject(); }
  } // no auth token, no session.
  // get the parts
  var sessionId = clientAuthTokenParts[ 0 ],
  authToken = clientAuthTokenParts[ 1 ];
  // ask the database via dbutils if the token is recognized
  self._dbUtils.execute(
  "CALL tasker.security.verify_token (:1, :2, :3, :4, :5 )
  INTO :6",
  [ sessionId,
  authToken, // authorization token
  self._dbUtils.outVarchar2( { size: 32 } ),
  self._dbUtils.outVarchar2( { size: 4000 } ),
  self._dbUtils.outVarchar2( { size: 4000 } ),
  self._dbUtils.outVarchar2( { size: 1 } )
  ] )
  .then( function ( results ) {
    // returnParam3 has a Y or N; Y is good auth
```

```
        if ( results.returnParam3 === "Y" ) {
          // notify callback of successful auth
          var user = {
            userId:    results.returnParam, sessionId: sessionId,
            nextToken: results.returnParam1,
            hmacSecret: results.returnParam2
          };
          if ( cb ) { cb( null, user ) }
          else { deferred.resolve( user ); }
        } else {
          // auth failed
          if ( cb ) { cb( null, false ); } else { deferred.reject(); }
        }
      } )
      .catch( function ( err ) {
        if ( cb ) { return cb( err, false ); }
        else { deferred.reject(); }
      } )
      .done();
      if ( !cb ) { return deferred.promise; }
    };
```

The dbUtils.execute() method is a wrapper method around the Oracle query method we covered in the *Executing queries* section.

Once a session has been retrieved from the database, Passport will want to serialize the user. This is usually just the user's ID, but we serialize a little more (which, from the preceding code, is the user's ID, session ID, and the HMAC secret):

```
passport.serializeUser(function( user, done ) {
  done (null, user);
});
```

The serializeUser method is called after a successful authentication and it must be present, or an error will occur. There's also a deserializeUser method if you're using typical Passport sessions: this method is designed to restore the user information from the Passport session.

Before any of this will work, we also need to tell Express to use the Passport middleware:

```
app.use ( passport.initialize() );
```

Passport makes handling authentication simple, but it also provides session support as well. While we don't use it for Tasker, you can use it to support a typical session-based username/password authentication system quite easily with a single line of code:

```
app.use ( passport.session() );
```

 If you're intending to use sessions with Passport, make sure you also provide a `deserializeUser` method.

Next, we need to implement the code to authenticate a user with their username and password. Remember, we initially require the user to log in using their username and password, and once authenticated, we handle all further requests using tokens. To do this, we need to write a portion of our API code.

Building API handlers

We won't cover the entire API in this section, but we will cover a couple of small pieces, especially as they pertain to authentication and retrieving data.

First, we've codified our API in `/tasker-srv/api-def` in the code package for this book. You'll also want to take a look at `/tasker-srv/api-utils` to see how we parse out this data structure into useable routes for the Express router.

Basically, we codify our API by building a simple structure:

```
[ { "route": "/auth", "actions": [ … ] },
  { "route": "/task", "actions": [ … ] },
  { "route": "/task/{:taskId}", "params": [ … ],
  "actions": [ … ] },
  … ]
```

Each route can have any number of actions and parameters. Parameters are equivalent to the Express Router's parameters. In the preceding example, `{:taskId}` is a parameter that will take on the value of whatever is in that particular location in the URI. For example, `/task/21` will result in `taskId` with the value of 21. This is useful for our actions because each action can then assume that the parameters have already been parsed, so any actions on the `/task/{:taskId}` route will already have task information at hand.

The parameters are defined as follows:

```
{ "name": "taskId", "type": "number",
  "description": "…",
  "returns": [ … ],
  "securedBy": "tasker-auth",
  "handler": function (req, res, next, taskId) {…} }
```

Actions are defined as follows:

```
{ "title": "Task",
  "action": "get-task", "verb": "get",
  "description": { … },    // hypermedia description
  "returns": [ … ],        // http status codes that are returned
  "example": { … },        // example response
  "href": "/task/{taskId}", "template": true,
  "accepts": [ "application/json", … ],
  "sends": [ "application/json", … ],
  "securedBy": "tasker-auth", "hmac": "tasker-256",
  "store": { … }, "query-parameters": { … },
  "handler": function ( req, res, next ) { … } }
```

Each handler is called whenever that particular route is accessed by a client using the correct HTTP verbs (identified by `verb` in the prior code). This allows us to write a handler for each specific state transition in our API, which is nicer than having to write a large method that's responsible for the entire route. It also makes describing the API using hypermedia that much simpler, since we can require a portion of the API and call a simple utility method (`/tasker-srv/api-utils/index.js`) to generate the description for the client.

Since we're still working on how to handle authentication, here's how the API definition for the POST `/auth` route looks (the complete version is located at `/tasker-srv/api-def/auth/login.js`):

```
action = {
  "title": "Authenticate User",
  "action": "login",
  "description": [ … ], "example":      { … },
  "returns":      {
    200: "User authenticated; see information in body.",
    401: "Incorrect username or password.", …
  },
  "verb": "post", "href": "/auth",
  "accepts": [ "application/json", … ],
```

```
"sends": [ "application/json", … ],
"csrf": "tasker-csrf",
"store": {
  "body": [ { name: "session-id", key: "sessionId" },
  { name: "hmac-secret", key: "hmacSecret" },
  { name: "user-id", key: "userId" },
  { name: "next-token", key: "nextToken" } ]
},
"template": {
  "user-id": {
    "title": "User Name", "key": "userId",
    "type": "string", "required": true,
    "maxLength": 32, "minLength": 1
  },
  "candidate-password": {
    "title": "Password", "key": "candidatePassword",
    "type": "string", "required": true,
    "maxLength": 255, "minLength": 1
  }
},
```

The earlier code is largely documentation (but it is returned to the client when they request this resource). The following code handler is what actually performs the authentication:

```
"handler": function ( req, res, next ) {
  var session = new Session( new DBUtils(
  req.app.get( "client-pool" ) ) ),
    username,
    password;
  // does our input validate?
  var validationResults =
  objUtils.validate( req.body, action.template );
  if ( !validationResults.validates ) {
    return next(
    Errors.HTTP_Bad_Request( validationResults.message ) );
  }
  // got here -- good; copy the values out
  username = req.body.userId;
  password = req.body.candidatePassword;
  //  create a session with the username and password
  session.createSession( username, password )
    .then( function ( results ) {
      // no session? bad username or password
```

```
          if ( !results ) {
            return next( Errors.HTTP_Unauthorized() );
          }
        // return the session information to the client
        var o = {
          sessionId: results.sessionId,
          hmacSecret: results.hmacSecret,
          userId:    results.userId,
          nextToken: results.nextToken,
          _links:    {}, _embedded: {}
        };
        // generate hypermedia
        apiUtils.generateHypermediaForAction(
        action, o._links, security, "self" );
          [ require( "../task/getTaskList" ),
            require( "../task/getTask" ),   …
            require( "../auth/logout" )
          ].forEach( function ( apiAction ) {
              apiUtils.generateHypermediaForAction(
              apiAction, o._links, security );
          } );
          resUtils.json( res, 200, o );
        } )
        .catch( function ( err ) {
          return next( err );
          } )
        .done();
      }
    };
```

The session.createSession method looks very similar to session.findSession, as shown in the following code:

```
  Session.prototype.createSession =
  function ( userName, candidatePassword, cb ) {
    var self = this,
    deferred = Q.defer();
    if ( typeof userName === "undefined" ||
    typeof candidatePassword === "undefined" ) {
      if ( cb ) { return cb( null, false ); }
      else { deferred.reject(); }
    }
    // attempt to authenticate
    self._dbUtils.execute(
```

```
"CALL tasker.security.authenticate_user( :1, :2, :3," +
" :4, :5 ) INTO :6", [
userName, candidatePassword,
self._dbUtils.outVarchar2( { size: 4000 },
self._dbUtils.outVarchar2( { size: 4000 } ),
self._dbUtils.outVarchar2( { size: 4000 } ),
self._dbUtils.outVarchar2( { size: 1 } ] )
.then( function ( results ) {
  // ReturnParam3 has Y or N; Y is good auth
  if ( results.returnParam3 === "Y" ) {
    // notify callback of auth info
    var user = {
      userId:    userName,
      sessionId: results.returnParam,
      nextToken: results.returnParam1,
      hmacSecret: results.returnParam2
    };
    if ( cb ) { cb( null, user ); }
    else { deferred.resolve( user ); }
  } else {
    // auth failed
    if ( cb ) { cb( null, false ); }
    else { deferred.reject(); }
  }
} )
.catch( function ( err ) {
  if ( cb ) { return cb( err, false ) }
  else { deferred.reject(); }
} )
.done();
if ( !cb ) { return deferred.promise; }
};
```

Once the API is fully codified, we need to go back to `app.js` and tell Express that it should use the API's routes:

```
app.use ( "/", apiUtils.createRouterForApi(apiDef, checkAuth));
```

We also add a global variable so that whenever an API section needs to return the entire API as a hypermedia structure, it can do so without traversing the entire API again:

```
app.set( "x-api-root", apiUtils.generateHypermediaForApi(
apiDef, securityDef ) );
```

The `checkAuth` method shown previously is pretty simple; all it does is ensure that we don't authenticate more than once in a single request:

```
function checkAuth ( req, res, next ) {
  if (req.isAuthenticated()) {
    return next();
  }
  passport.authenticate ( "req" )(req, res, next);
}
```

You might be wondering where we're actually forcing our handlers to use authentication. There's actually a bit of magic in `/tasker-srv/api-utils`. I've highlighted the relevant portions:

```
createRouterForApi:function (api, checkAuthFn) {
  var router = express.Router();
  // process each route in the api; a route consists of the
  // uri (route) and a series of verbs (get, post, etc.)
  api.forEach ( function ( apiRoute ) {
    // add params
    if ( typeof apiRoute.params !== "undefined" ) {
      apiRoute.params.forEach ( function ( param ) {
        if (typeof param.securedBy !== "undefined" ) {
          router.param( param.name, function ( req, res,
          next, v) {
            return checkAuthFn( req, res,
            param.handler.bind(this, req, res, next, v) );
          });
        } else {
          router.param(param.name, param.handler);
        }
      });
    }
    var uri = apiRoute.route;
    // create a new route with the uri
    var route = router.route ( uri );
    // process through each action
    apiRoute.actions.forEach ( function (action) {
      // just in case we have more than one verb, split them out
      var verbs = action.verb.split(",");
      // and add the handler specified to the route
      // (if it's a valid verb)
      verbs.forEach ( function (verb) {
        if (typeof route[verb] === "function") {
```

```
        if (typeof action.securedBy !== "undefined") {
          route[verb]( checkAuthFn, action.handler );
        } else {
          route[verb]( action.handler );
        }
      }
    });
  });
 });
 return router;
};
```

Once you've finished writing even a few handlers, you should be able to verify that the system works by posting requests to your API. First, make sure your server has started ; we use the following code line to start the server:

```
export NODE_ENV=development; npm start
```

For some of the routes, you could just load up a browser and point it at your server. If you type `https://localhost:4443/` in your browser, you should see a response that looks a lot like this:

```
"version": "Tasker API v0.1",
"toPOST": [
    "In order to POST, you'll need to get a token via get-token. You'll also",    ],
    "need to support cookies in order to support CSRF tokens."

"toAUTH": [
    "In order to authenticate, first get a token from get-token, then",           ],
    "call login with the user id and candidate password. If invalid 401 Unauthorized",
    "is returned, otherwise a session is returned. Use nextToken and send",
    "that token on the next request. If nextToken is null, preserve the prior",
    "token."

"info": [
    "This API is a sample API for the PhoneGap Enterprise book published",        ],
    "by Packt Publishing and written by Kerri Shotts. For more information",
    "please visit the website for the book at ",
    "http://www.photokandy.com/books/phonegap-enterprise"

"_links": {
                          "self": {                                              },
                                   "title": "API Discovery",
                                   "action": "discover_api",
                                   "description": "Returns all the valid API actions",
                                   "returns": {                                   },
                                              "200": "OK"

                                   "verb": "get",
                                   "href": "/",
                                   "base-href": "/",
                                   "accepts": [                                    ],
                                              "application/hal+json",
                                              "application/json",
                                              "text/json"

                                   "sends": [                                      ]
                                            "application/hal+json",
                                            "application/json",
                                            "text/json"
```

If you're thinking this looks styled, you're right. The Tasker API generates responses based on the client's requested format. The browser requests data in HTML, and so our API generates a styled HTML page as a response. For an app, the response is JSON because the app requests that the response be in JSON. If you want to see how this works, see / `tasker-srv/res-utils/index.js`.

If you want to actually send and receive data, though, you'll want to get a REST client rather than using the browser. There are many good free clients: Firefox has a couple of good clients as does Chrome. Or you can find a native client for your operating system. You'll find a few interesting clients in the *RESTful-like API Resources* section in *Appendix, Useful Resources*.

Although you can do everything with `curl` on the command prompt, RESTful clients are much easier to use and often offer useful features, such as dynamic variables, various authentication methods built in, and many can act as simple automated testers.

Summary

In this chapter, we've covered how to build a web server that bridges the gap between our database backend and our mobile application. We've provided an overview of RESTful-like APIs, and we've also quickly shown how to implement such a web API using Node.js. We've also covered authentication and session handling using Passport.

In the next chapter, we'll start working on our PhoneGap app, primarily by verifying that it can properly communicate with our new web API. It won't be pretty yet, that's for a later chapter, but it will be able to authenticate and list tasks.

5
Communicating between Mobile and the Middle-Tier

To this point, we've largely focused on various security concerns and the backend systems, and much of what we've discussed applies to applications on any platform and not just those developed on PhoneGap. In this chapter, however, we'll cover the creation of a new mobile app that can communicate with the backend we've built.

In this chapter, we'll focus on the following points:

- A brief look at **Promises**
- Verifying that the communication channel is secure
- Using XMLHttpRequest to communicate with the backend RESTful-like API
- Authenticating the end user with the backend

Getting started

It's easy to use our sample project for this chapter rather than trying to build something from scratch. You can find this under the /ch5 directory in the code package for this project.

If you want to create a new Cordova project using our project as a base, use a command like the following:

```
cordova create ./your-directory com.packtpub.pgech5 TaskerCH5 --copy-from
./ch5
```

Then, add the following plugin (for SSL Certificate pinning):

```
cordova plugin add https://github.com/EddyVerbruggen/
SSLCertificateChecker-PhoneGap-Plugin.git
```

The project uses `https://localhost:4443` as the base URI; you'll want to change this to point at your server. This can be configured by modifying `www/js/app/main.js`. Look for the `baseURI` variable (around line 121) and modify as appropriate. Once done, you should be able to run the app on your device using one of the following command lines:

```
cordova run platform-name # ios or android
```

```
cordova emulate platform-name
```

There are a lot of files that are contained within the project, most of which don't really do anything right now. The important files are as follows:

- `www/index.html`: This is the initial web page loaded by Cordova, which includes content-security policy META tags.

- `www/app/main.js`: This is the bulk of our demo. It checks if the SSL connection is secure. If so, it fires off a series of **XHRs**.

- `www/app/lib/xhr.js`: This is a simple XHR library that supports automatic retries. It utilizes Promises exclusively.

- `www/app/lib/objUtils.js`: These are utilities we use to manipulate objects.

- `www/app/lib/hateoas.js`: This is a simple library that makes working with HATEOAS-compliant RESTful-like APIs easier.

- `www/app/lib/cryptojs.js`: This is a third-party library that provides PBKDF2 support.

- `www/app/models/session.js`: This is a simple session model.

 One other important note: when using a content-security policy in a Cordova app, be sure to include `gap://*` as a valid source, or your app might not be able to interface with plugins. Our demo includes this on the `www/index.html` page.

Promises

Before we go any further, it's important that you understand the concept of Promises. You can find the specification for Promises at http://promisesaplus.com if you want to read it, but in short, Promises allow us to avoid *callback hell* when working with asynchronous operations. Because every request we make to a Cordova plugin or to our backend via XHR (XMLHttpRequest) is asynchronous and requires callbacks, it would be very easy to descend into an unmaintainable mess of spaghetti code.

The callback pattern looks like the following:

```
doSomethingAsync ( function ( results ) {
  // do something with results
});
```

While this isn't terribly hard to understand when we're only using one level of callback, it can quickly escalate, as in the following:

```
step1 ( function ( results ) {
  step2 ( function ( results ) {
    step3 ( function ( results ) {
      step4 ( function ( results ) {
        ...
      })
    })
  })
})
```

Should the methods require multiple callbacks (perhaps one for a success callback and another in the case of an error), it gets even messier.

Promises, on the other hand, enable code that looks like the following:

```
step1().then (step2)
       .then (step3)
       .then (step4)...
       .catch ( function(err) { console.log (err); } )
       .done ();
```

In practice, the code is rarely this clean; however, this is a good illustration.

A Promise is really quite simple; it's a promise that we'll eventually resolve an asynchronous request to a value sometime down the road. When we do, we'll call the next method in the Promise chain. If an error occurs, we'll call the next catch method in the chain instead.

ECMAScript 6 (ES6) contains native support for Promises. Unfortunately, it isn't widely supported by mobile platforms yet. Instead, we must rely on a library that implements promises. I use **Q**; you are welcome to use whatever promise library you prefer as they all work in a similar way. If you want to download Q, you can find it at `https://github.com/kriskowal/q`. We have included a version in the code package for this book.

Unfortunately, we can't cover everything about Promises in this book. However, if you want to learn more, **HTML5 Rocks** has a fantastic example about the use of **ES6** promises at `http://www.html5rocks.com/en/tutorials/es6/promises/`.

Ensuring secure communication

As we discussed in *Chapter 3, Securing PhoneGap Apps,* the best way to ensure that communication with the backend is secure is to use SSL Certificate pinning. Prior to every request, we verify that the certificate being utilized to secure communications is a known certificate.

We're using a plugin developed by Eddy Verbruggen called **SSLCertificateChecker**. To add this to a Cordova project, refer to *Chapter 3, Securing Phonegap Apps,* or the *Getting Started* section in this chapter.

We covered a very simple example in *Chapter 3, Securing PhoneGap Apps.* Unfortunately, that particular sample relied solely on callbacks, it would have been better if the sample was wrapped with a Promise instead, as in the following code:

```
function _checkIfSecure( server, fingerprints ) {
  var deferred = Q.defer();
  try {
    var args = [];
    // success
    args.push( function success( message ) {
      deferred.resolve( message );
    } );
    // failure
    args.push( function failure( message ) {
      deferred.reject( message );
    } );
    // server
    args.push( server );
    // fingerprints
    for ( var i = 0; i < fingerprints.length; i++ ) {
      args.push( fingerprints[ i ] );
```

```
    }
    window.plugins.sslCertificateChecker.check.apply( this,
    args );
  } catch ( err ) {
    // if window.plugins isn't defined, we'll go ahead
    // and resolve instead
    if ( typeof window.plugins === "undefined" ) {
      deferred.resolve( "" );
    } else {
      deferred.reject( err );
    }
  }
  return deferred.promise;
}
```

Wrapping a Promise using Q is very simple: the function creates a deferred (asynchronous) Promise by calling `Q.defer`. At the end of the function, the deferred Promise is returned (`deferred.promise`).

Perhaps the hardest part to understand about Promises is that the function always returns well in advance before completing the asynchronous task. This means that if you call a function that returns a Promise, control is returned immediately, and the calling function is not paused just because a Promise is pending. The value that is returned is an object *representing a Promise* and not the actual value because it hasn't yet been determined.

The asynchronous activity finishes at some later time, and at this point we can resolve the Promise. If the activity finished successfully, we call `deferred.resolve` with the value. This will then call the next item (indicated by `then`) in the Promise chain with the resolved value (whatever this might be). However, if the activity fails, we call `deferred.reject` with a value representing the error. Furthermore, control gets passed to the next `catch` handler in the chain, if available. If none are available, you'll see an unhandled exception in the web console.

The reason we're going through all this effort is because the SSL Certificate Checker plugin is asynchronous, meaning we can't call the `check` routine and immediately know if the connection is safe or not. Instead, we have to wait for the request to be made; at this point, we'll be notified if the connection is secure.

We're also calling the check routine very differently than we did in *Chapter 3, Securing PhoneGap Apps*. The main reason for this is that the check routine allows us to pass one or two SSL Certificate fingerprints, and there's no sense in writing code for both scenarios, which will largely be duplicate work. Instead, we construct the arguments to the method dynamically. If there's only one fingerprint, the args array comes out with four parameters: the success method (which calls deferred. resolve), the failure method (which calls deferred.reject), the server URI, and the single fingerprint. However, if there are two (or more) fingerprints, we'll have a longer list. (Right now, the plugin only accepts up to two fingerprints, but it is possible this could change in the future.)

In order to call the check method with this list of arguments, we can use apply. The first argument to apply is actually the object that should represent this, not the first parameter to check. The second argument is an array of items that should be passed in as arguments to the function. The first item in the array corresponds to the first argument expected by the function, and so on.

With this function already written, we can use it as follows:

```
checkIfSecured ( "https://www.example.com:1234",
[ someSSLCertificateFingerprint, anotherFingerprint ] )
then ( function (msg) {
  // continue with communication
})
.catch ( function (err) {
  // NOT secure! (err=CONNECTION_NOT_SECURE)
  // or NO internet connection (err=CONNECTION_FAILED)
})
.done();
```

Before we continue, we need to mention that this method isn't as secure as true SSL Certificate Pinning. To be truly secure, the certificate must be checked on *every* communication attempt. You can write code that checks every time, but there's one other reason why this isn't as secure: the fingerprint is in your JavaScript code.

If you remember in *Chapter 3, Securing PhoneGap Apps*, your JavaScript code is human-readable and world-accessible. This means that an attacker can modify the fingerprint such that it will permit their SSL Certificate, but not your own, and the user of the attacker's app will not know the difference. Or worse, the attacker might be able to construct a different SSL Certificate that matches your fingerprint, thus allowing them to perform a man-in-the middle attack without your users being aware of it.

The only way to increase the security is to use a plugin that checks the entire certificate as a whole and not just the fingerprint, and this also requires backend requests to pass through the security plugin. Whereas most web apps will use WebSockets or XMLHttpRequest to communicate with the backend, such a security plugin would require that such requests go through it instead (for example, SSLChecker. makeGetRequest (...)). Such a plugin is available, but we aren't using it in our code because it doesn't yet support all available HTTP methods (just GET and POST). If you're curious, it's available at https://github.com/wymsee/cordova-HTTP.

Communicating with the backend using XHR

Most of the time, you'll want to communicate with your backend server by using XMLHttpRequest to send and receive JSON-formatted data. From now on, we'll use XHR as an abbreviation for this term.

XHR was designed by Microsoft in order to allow web applications to communicate with other servers and increase web app dynamism and responsiveness. XHR was later implemented by other browser vendors, and it eventually became a W3C standard.

The first version of XHR was amazing for the time, but it became apparent that additional flexibility was needed, and so XHR level 2 (XHR2) was created. Built on the original standard, XHR2 increased security by providing support for cross-domain requests using **Cross-Origin Resource Sharing** (**CORS**). It also enhanced XHR's flexibility by allowing many more data types to be sent and received.

A very simple XHR request looks like the following:

```
var xhr = new XMLHttpRequest();
xhr.open ( "GET", "http://www.example.com/api/getPeople", true );
xhr.onload = function (e) {
  if (this.status === 200) {
    var people = JSON.parse (this.responseText);
  } else {
    // an HTTP error occurred
  }
}
xhr.send(null);
```

An XHR request is processed as follows:

- The XHR request is created (new XMLHttpRequest()).
- The XHR request is opened (open), this specifies the HTTP method that will be used (GET, POST, DELETE, PUT, and so on) and the URI. It also indicates if the request will be asynchronous (true as the third parameter) or not (false as the third parameter). Although it is possible to create synchronous XHRs, it is highly unadvisable as this blocks your web app until the XHR is resolved.
- An onload handler is defined, which indicates how we'll respond to the XHR response.
- The request is sent.
- When the response has been completely loaded, the onload handler is called with the response.
- The onload handler processes the results.

Should it be necessary to respond to other conditions beyond the completion of the request, additional handlers can be added to the XHR as follows:

- ontimeout: This is called when the XHR request times out (the timeout delay is determined by setting xhr.timeout).
- onerror: This is called when the XHR request encounters an error (for example, in the case of an unreachable server).
- onreadystatechange: This is called when the state of the XHR changes. Valid values are:
  - 0 (unopened): This XHR has not yet been opened
  - 1 (unsent): This XHR has not yet been sent
  - 2 (headers_received): This XHR has been sent, and headers have been received (but has no body content yet)
  - 3 (loading): This XHR has been sent, headers have been received, and some body content is available
  - 4 (done): This XHR is complete
- onloadstart: This is called when the XHR actually starts
- onloadend: This is called when the XHR completes (in success or failure)
- onabort: This is called when the XHR was aborted
- onprogress: This is called to indicate the progress of the request

For unsecured resources, a simple XHR is sufficient. However, for our API, we'll need a more complex XHR. If you recall, we have a couple of layers of security, as follows:

- Secured resources expect a valid token in the headers, and this token changes with each secured request.

- Requests that change content (PUT, POST, DELETE, and so on) require a CSRF token passed in the header. This includes logging in, since this is a POST to /auth.

- Secured resources also expect an HMAC to verify that the message hasn't been modified in transit.

CSRF tokens are pretty easy to handle, since they are easily managed with cookies. In order to enable an XHR to send and receive cookies, we just set withCredentials to true, as follows:

```
xhr.withCredentials = true;
```

When it comes to running your app in the browser, this might fail if the browser is rejecting third-party cookies. At the moment, this occurs with Safari and Mobile Safari, but I would expect Firefox and Chrome to eventually follow suit. PhoneGap is not impacted by this; since code runs locally, it isn't subject to the same-origin policy.

Note that this doesn't actually send the CSRF token in the headers; it just allows us to send and receive the session cookie that the server uses to ensure we respond with the correct CSRF token. To add the header, we can call setRequestHeader prior to sending the XHR:

```
xhr.setRequestHeader ("x-csrf-token", csrfToken);
```

If you're dealing with an API that is secured using HTTP Basic Authentication, you can also use XHR to pass the username and password easily. Just supply these as the fourth and fifth parameters to xhr.open, respectively:

```
xhr.open ( method, URI, true, username, password );
```

If you find the username/password not being sent, you can send it using a request header:
```
xhr.setRequestHeader("Authorization", "Basic " +
btoa(username + ":" + password));
```

In our API's case, security is handled with tokens, and as such, they need to be sent via a header, which is why our demo only uses three parameters and sends the following header instead:

```
xhr.setRequestHeader ("x-auth-token", authToken);
```

Of course, one must obtain these tokens prior to sending them. This means that any HTTP request that changes content (POST, PUT, DELETE, and so on) will first have to make a GET request in order to obtain a session cookie and a CSRF token. In our API, this will be a GET request to /csrf, and the token will be returned in the body as follows:

```
{
    token: "abcdefg-hijklmnop-12305859",
    ...
}
```

It should be obvious by now that we'll need to chain many XHR requests together, and building each of them in the preceding manner will be time-consuming, repetitive, and error prone. To this end, we developed a very simple XHR library that works with Promises and provides automatic retry support. We won't show the code in the text, but if you want to see it in full, look at /ch5/www/js/app/lib/xhr.js.

This library makes it very simple to chain XHR requests together, as follows:

```
XHR.send ("GET", "https://pge-as.example.com:4443/csrf")
.then ( function ( response ) {
  return XHR.send ("POST",
  "https://pge-as.example.com:4443/auth",{
  data: { userId: "BSMITH", candidatePassword: "password" },
  headers: [ { headerName: "x-csrf-token",
  headerValue: response.token } ] } )
})
.then ( function ( response ) {
  ...
})
.catch ( function (err) {
  ...
})
.done();
```

At this point, you're officially communicating with the server! Unfortunately, any code you write will be highly coupled with this particular version of the API and its associated URIs. If you're fine with this, that's OK, in many ways it's *faster* to write code that is highly coupled with the API. However, if you want a more loosely coupled client, we should discuss how best to deal with a RESTful-like API that also embodies **Hypermedia As The Engine Of Application State (HATEOAS)**.

With such an API, the response is likely to look something like the following:

```
{
  "field1": "value1",
  "field2": "value2",
  "_links": {
    "self": {
      "href": "/collection/21"
    },
    "get-comments": {
        "href": "/collection/21/comments"
    }
  }
}
```

In this case, the response is providing us additional information about the resource we've obtained. We can access the resource again by visiting /collection/21 (the self link) and we can access the comments on the resource by visiting /collection/21/comments. In the real world, the response is likely to be quite a bit larger and indicate even more actions that can occur.

Immediately, we can see that we should avoid hardcoding URIs if at all possible. Instead, we should ask the API what URI it prefers to use for a given action. We're still somewhat coupled to the API based on the name of the action, but the API can change the URI format at any time without breaking our code.

Typically, as shown in the following code, we ask the API what we can do by making a GET request to the root of the API (this is called API discovery):

```
XHR.send ( "GET", baseURI + "/")
```

Let's look at a small portion of the response we receive from our API:

```
{{
  "version": "Tasker API v0.1",
  "toPOST": [ "In order to POST, …", … ],
  "toAUTH": [ "In order to authenticate, …", … ],
  "info": [ "This API is a sample API for…", … ],
  "_links": {
    "get-csrf-token": {
      "title": "Get CSRF Token",
      "action": "get-csrf-token",
      "description": [ "Returns a token…", … ],
      "example": {"body": { "token": "csrf-token" } },
      "returns": { "200": "OK" },
      "verb": "get",
      "href": "/csrf",
      "accepts": [ "application/json", … ],
      "sends": [ "application/json", … ],
      "store": { "body": [ {
        "name": "csrf-token", "key": "token"
      } ]
    },
    "allow": "get"
  },
  "login": {
    "title": "Authenticate User",
    "action": "login",
    "description": [ "Authenticates a user…", …],
    "example": { "body": {
      "sessionId": "92013",
      "hmacToken": "AABBCCDDEEFF11223344556677889900",
      "userId": "BMSITH",
      "nextToken": "0099887766554433221100AABBCCDDEE"
    } },
    "returns": {
      "200": "User authenticated; see information in body.", …
    },
    "verb": "post",
    "href": "/auth",
    "accepts": [ … ],
    "sends": [ … ],
    "csrf": "tasker-csrf",
    "store": { "body": [
```

```
          { "name": "session-id", "key": "sessionId" }, … ]
        },
        "template": {
          "user-id": {
            "title": "User Name", "key": "userId",
            "type": "string", "required": true,
            "maxLength": 32, "minLength": 1
          },
          "candidate-password": {
            "title": "Password", "key": "candidatePassword",
            "type": "string", "required": true,
            "maxLength": 255, "minLength": 1
          }
        },
        "allow": "post",
        "csrf-action": [ "get-csrf-token" ],
        "attachments": {
          "headers": [ {
            "name": "csrf-token", "key": "x-csrf-token",
          "value": "{csrf-token}", "templated": true } ]
        }
      }, …
    }
  }
```

You can already see that the response includes more than just links to other resources. This also includes information about what headers are expected for a request as well as what fields should be included when sending a POST to a URI.

Given the preceding information, it's possible to construct an XHR chain that doesn't have any URI, JSON format, and headers hardcoded (other than the base URI). It's possible to make a library that abstracts all of this away, but this is well out of the scope of this book.

Instead, we'll construct some helper methods that lets us get close without actually having to implement a finite state automaton (state machine) and a domain-specific language (DSL) parser.

First, we're going to need a method to handle values that are marked as templated in the preceding response. These might be URIs (/task/{taskId}) or header values ({session-id}.{next-token}). We'll assume that these values are being stored to a shared context object. This makes the code fairly simple:

```
function interpolate( str, context ) {
  var newStr = str;
  if ( typeof context === "undefined" ) {
    return newStr;
  }
  str.match( /\{([^\}]+)\}/g ).forEach( function ( match ) {
    var prop = match.substr( 1, match.length - 2 ).trim();
    newStr = newStr.replace( match,
    valueForKeyPath( context, prop ) );
  } );
  return newStr;
}
```

The preceding code does depend on another function: valueForKeyPath. This function looks like the following, and lets us drill down into an object using a string like field1.field2[index3] without worrying if there is a null or undefined value along the way.

```
function valueForKeyPath( o, k, d ) {
  if ( o === undefined || o === null ) {
    return ( d !== undefined ) ? d : o;
  }
  var v = o;
  v = k.match( /([\w\$\\\-]+)/g ).reduce( function ( v,keyPart ) {
    if ( v === undefined || v === null ) { return v; }
    try {
      return v[ keyPart ];
    } catch ( err ) {
      return undefined;
    }
  }, v );
  return ( ( v === undefined || v === null ) &&
  ( d !== undefined ) ) ? d : v;
}
```

What interpolate does is first find all the text wrapped with braces ({ and }). For each instance, we obtain the associated value in context. In a small way, it's like a templating method.

Let's assume that `context` looks like the following:

```
{ "taskId": 21, "somethingElse": "hi!",
"task": { "title": "bar" } }
```

Calling `interpolate` with a string of `{taskId}/{somethingElse},{task.title}` will result in the following response:

```
21/hi!,bar
```

Next, we need to create a method that will store individual pieces of data from the response that the API indicates we need to keep. In the preceding API response, this is indicated by a `store` entry in the response:

```
function storeResponseToContext( r, context ) {
  var selfStore =
  ObjUtils.valueForKeyPath(r,"body._links.self.store" );
  if ( selfStore === undefined ) { return; }
  Object.keys( selfStore )
  .forEach( function ( prop ) {
    var o = selfStore[ prop ];
    o.forEach( function ( item ) {
      context[ item.name ] =
      ObjUtils.valueForKeyPath( r[ prop ], item.key );
    } );
  } );
}
```

It's guaranteed that the response will have a `self` link, and this link will include a list of all the items we need to store. Let's say the response includes the following in the `self` link:

```
"store": { "body": [ { "name": "csrf-token", "key": "token" }
] }
```

Let's also say that the body of the response looks partly like this:

```
{ token: "abcdef", … }
```

Then, if we call `storeResponseToContext`, we'll end up with our `context` that looks like this object:

```
{ "csrf-token": "abcdef" }
```

At this point, our code can then extract the contents of the data in a loosely coupled fashion. It only needs to know that the CSRF token is always represented in the context by the `csrf-token` key, but it doesn't need to know how it is represented in the actual response because the response tells us exactly how to extract it. The API can be changed such that if the `token` was renamed to `gobbledygook`, then our code can still access it in the `context` via `csrf-token`.

When it comes to sending a response, the API also tells us what data it wants, and the format of that data. It does so via a `template` property:

```
"template": {
  "user-id": {
    "title": "User Name", "key": "userId",
    "type": "string", "required": true,
    "maxLength": 32, "minLength": 1
  },
  "candidate-password": {
    "title": "Password", "key": "candidatePassword",
    "type": "string", "required": true,
    "maxLength": 255, "minLength": 1
  }
}
```

In order to construct a proper response, we'll create an object containing the fields we know that we need to send, and then map our keys to the keys the API expects:

```
function map( o, usingTemplate ) {
  var newO = {};
  Object.keys( usingTemplate )
    .forEach( function ( prop ) {
      var v = usingTemplate[ prop ];
      if ( o[ prop ] !== undefined ) {
        newO[ v.key ] = o[ prop ];
      }
    } );
  return newO;
}
```

If we want to construct a login request with the proper JSON format, we can now use the following code:

```
var postData = map ({ "user-id": "JDOE",
"candidate-password": "password" }, template );
```

`postdata` will look like this object:

```
{ "userId": "JDOE", "candidatePassword": "password" }
```

Again, we're still coupled to the API, but we're *not* highly coupled to specific field names in JSON. Since the API tells us that it wants the `user-id` to be sent with the field name of `userId` in JSON, we can construct exactly the correct response. However, if the API had wanted it as `username` instead, our code wouldn't have to change at all.

We're not quite ready yet to actually send a request; we might have headers we need to send. This is indicated in the API with an `attachments` item:

```
"attachments": {
  "headers": [
    { "name": "csrf-token", "key": "x-csrf-token",
      "value": "{csrf-token}", "templated": true } ]
}
```

We can build the correct headers using the following code:

```
function buildHeadersAttachment( headers, context ) {
  var returnHeaders = [];
  if ( typeof headers === "undefined" ) {
    return returnHeaders;
  }
  headers.forEach( function ( header ) {
    if ( typeof header.templated ===
    "undefined" || !header.templated ) {
      returnHeaders.push(
      { headerName: header.key, headerValue: header.value } );
      } else {
      returnHeaders.push( { headerName: header.key,
      headerValue: ObjUtils.interpolate( header.value,
      context ) } );
    }
  } );
  return returnHeaders;
}
```

If you remember our `context` from a few pages ago; if we call this method with the `headers` portion of the `attachments` item and the prior `context`, we'll receive the following object:

```
[ { headerName: "x-csrf-token",headerValue: "abcdef" } ]
```

Now that we've defined our headers and mapped the data, we need to send the format the API expects; we can make a request that isn't tightly coupled to the API:

```
return XHR.send ( r.body._links["login"].verb,
baseURI + r.body._links["login"].href,
{ data: postData, headers: headers } );
```

Notice that we don't even indicate the HTTP method; we let the API indicate this to us as well (look at the `verb` item in the response a few pages back). The URI we should use is also taken from the API response.

As we mentioned in *Chapter 3, Securing PhoneGap Apps*, we should also sign requests with a **Hashed Message Authentication Code (HMAC)**. This allows our backend to be reasonably sure that the message it received hasn't been altered while in transit. To craft an HMAC, one needs a shared secret as well as the HMAC format the backend expects. One also needs a crypto library in order to sign the message. We use CryptoJS, available at `https://code.google.com/p/crypto-js/`.

Our API defines its HMAC as follows:

```
{date:%Y%m%d.%H%M}.{route}{query-string}.{body}
```

We're not going to write code to parse this definition (you can do so if you'd like). So, in this case, we're going to be a little more tightly coupled to the API than we might like.

We still need the HMAC secret; this can be obtained in any number of ways, but in our demo app, the secret is obtained after a successful authentication with the server.

In *Chapter 3, Securing PhoneGap Apps*, we indicated that JavaScript Crypto is worthless. In our case, however, we aren't attempting to encrypt data in any form; we're just using cryptographic routines to perform hashes on a message in order to help verify integrity. Does this add a great deal of security? No, but it does require that the attacker know how our HMAC is constructed *and* have access to the HMAC secret in order to construct malicious messages.

Constructing an HMAC is pretty easy, but formatting the date and time is tough, as shown in the following code. Here's how:

```
function makeHMAC( url, body, context ) {
  function pad2( v ) {
    return ( v < 10 ) ? "0" + v : "" + v;
  }
  var now = new Date(), nowYYYY, nowMM, nowDD, nowHH,
  nowMI, dateString = "", stringToHmac = "",
  hmacString = "";
  now.setMinutes( now.getMinutes() );
  nowYYYY = now.getUTCFullYear();
  nowMM = now.getUTCMonth() + 1;
  nowDD = now.getUTCDate();
  nowHH = now.getUTCHours();
  nowMI = now.getUTCMinutes();
  dateString = "" + nowYYYY + pad2( nowMM ) + pad2( nowDD ) +
  "." + pad2( nowHH ) + pad2( nowMI );
  stringToHmac = "" + dateString + "." + url;
  if ( body !== undefined && body !== null ) {
    stringToHmac += JSON.stringify( body );
  }
  hmacString = CryptoJS.HmacSHA256( stringToHmac,
  context[ "hmac-secret" ] ).toString( CryptoJS.enc.Hex );
  context[ "hmac-token" ] = hmacString;
}
```

As long as the request specifies that it needs an HMAC token in the headers, `buildHeadersAttachment` will create the appropriate header.

 You must construct HMACs in the same way the server expects, or your HMAC won't match. Most servers will give a little bit of leeway with regard to time (ours allows the client to be within five minutes of the server), but the construction of the HMAC itself must match.

At this point, we can now construct an XHR chain that's simple to follow and remains loosely coupled from the API, as follows:

```
XHR.checkIfSecure( baseURI,
["27 02 A5 EB 95 91 41 66 C3 9F 82 D3 59 14 13 0E 13 B5 13 9E"] )
.then( function ( msg ) {
    return XHR.send( "GET", baseURI + "/" );
  } )
  .then( function ( r ) {
```

```
      console.log( "Response from API Discovery", r );
      return XHR.send( r.body._links[ "get-csrf-token" ].verb,
      baseURI + r.body._links[ "get-csrf-token" ].href );
  } )
  .then( function ( r ) {
      console.log( "Response from CSRF token request", r );
      Hateoas.storeResponseToContext( r, context );
      // create post response based upon the template
      var loginAction = r.body._links[ "login" ];
      var postData = Hateoas.map( {
        "user-id": "JDOE",
        "candidate-password": "password"
      }, loginAction.template );
      // build response headers
      var headers = Hateoas.buildHeadersAttachment(
      loginAction.attachments.headers, context );
      // send request
      return XHR.send( r.body._links[ "login" ].verb,
      baseURI + r.body._links[ "login" ].href, {
        data: postData,
        headers: headers
      } );
  } )
  .then( function ( r ) {
      console.log( r, "Response from AUTH POST" );
      Hateoas.storeResponseToContext( r, context );
      console.log( context, "Context after storing" );
      session = new Session( {
        sessionId: context[ "session-id" ],
        hmacSecret: context[ "hmac-secret" ],
        userId: context[ "user-id" ],
        nextToken: context[ "next-token" ]
      } );
      console.log( session, "Session after pulling from context" );
      var URI = ObjUtils.interpolate( r.body._links[
      "get-task" ].href, { "taskId": 2 } );
      makeHMAC( URI, undefined, context );
      var headers = Hateoas.buildHeadersAttachment(
      r.body._links[ "get-task" ].attachments.headers, context );
      return XHR.send( r.body._links[ "get-task" ].verb,
      baseURI + URI, {  headers: headers } );
  } )
  .then( function ( r ) {
      console.log( r, "Response from GET task" );
```

```
} )
.catch( function ( err ) {
  console.log( err, "failure in chain" );
} )
.done();
```

In practice, most XHR chains aren't going to be nearly this long, but it does show how one can follow the hypermedia the API provides at each response to an arbitrarily deep level.

 I don't personally suggest making XHR chains this long, assuming the API returns all available actions upon discovery (requesting the root directory), we can store these actions for later use. This plays a little loose with the concept of HATEOAS, but it's a nice tradeoff that allows our code to be somewhat loosely coupled, while also permitting any interaction with the backend (not just those interactions specified by the last response).

It takes a lot of work to make an app very loosely coupled to the backend API. There are *many* ways in which the previously shown XHR chain can be improved further and condensed into a library of its own. We'll leave that as a task for the reader.

Authenticating the user with the backend

If your API is using HTTP Basic Authentication, sending the username and password with each XHR request via the open method is sufficient. However, if your API (like ours) uses a different authentication mechanism, you'll need to handle this appropriately.

In our case, authentication is initially handled by calling the login method provided by our API. Since this requires a CSRF token, we also have to call `get-csrf-token`. Once the token is received, we then POST a response that contains the token in the header and the username and password in the body.

At this point, the server responds with either a 401 error (Unauthorized) or session information that we need to keep. The former indicates that the backend cannot authenticate the user, while the latter indicates that the server created a session for the user.

Once authenticated, additional requests send a token in the header (x-auth-token). This token is initially received from the login response data, but thereafter it's a part of each additional response as a header (x-next-token). At each request, the token is sent back as an x-auth-token header along with the session ID. An example token is as follows:

```
1050.654B329F59DE742536BF9A44D0DB2AE0BF45ECD8354AAB67D716B15705349
CA627B81AF0D498A0B29CAA841D842062A319A14A669AACC1E7DF45C05B9F6FFECAB
3490BC34630739C153D2B0A97882BF354D94D3706A8DC1C52E2CF2CE1E8D17AB97B9
AC8A1D1E7800A8086345785B47CC815992E9582CAAF147607253656616E6F5859899
4337F80B10C309B5F9D5E7E65074A6A73E7C84884C2078454306519E669675B4C05
0B6B23E7A73C17CD9E3FB3FCF3AB278775A7483ECFD5EF6EFF3C08E4955A072935
AB59B6DCCF8D93C45ED25D4F007A8760F4A13D8C6D71284FB2F1BC1A82E437064
A772CE8E20B0E64B9FE1FFD59F6E2FA8A6BD692AA0C804CD1
```

The initial portion (prior to the period) is the session ID, and the final portion is the authorization token. There are actually two parts contained within this token as well; the first half matches the server's token exactly, while the second half is different. The server then does additional work on the token, and then compares it to the value stored when the last request was received. If the token matches, the secured data is returned, and if it doesn't match, a suitable HTTP error is returned.

As long as we send the correct token for each request, the server will respond correctly. This means that the token is equivalent to the user's username and password, and it must be treated with similar respect. There's a large benefit to using a token; however, its lifetime is guaranteed to be shorter than that of the username/password combination (which can be forever), which is beneficial from a security perspective. This means that the token shouldn't be given out without care (since it provides the same privileges as the username/password combination), but if the token is compromised, it can be disabled.

Since the token is maintained on the server-side (this is what makes our API only RESTful-like), it is also important that requests are queued up and sent one by one. In our demo app for this chapter, this was trivial; we only made one request chain. In a real app, however, it will be possible to generate several XHR requests executing simultaneously. Since the token will immediately change to another value, all but one XHR request will be invalid. As such, a server-synchronized token bottlenecks performance as only one secured resource can be requested one at a time. Our final app will contain such a queue, but you might wish to take it on as a challenge before you reach the remaining chapters. Alternatively, you might prefer not to change the token on every request (which reduces the bottleneck), or you might wish to come up with some alternative method that can be computed both on the client and the backend.

Summary

In this chapter, we briefly touched on Promises and how to verify our communication with the backend was secure. We explored communicating with our API using XMLHttpRequest in-depth and also discussed how to decouple our app from the API and instead allow the API responses to tell our app what it can do next. This means that as long as the client app respects the API contract, the underlying URIs, field names, templates, headers, and so on, can change and our code will execute without a problem.

At the end of the chapter, we addressed how our API handles authentication, and how tokens are converted from an intermediate form to a final form that the server will accept.

If you run our sample app on your device, you should see the output similar to the following screenshot:

In the next chapter, we'll cover handling application and network events, local storage options, encrypted storage options, and data caching and synchronization.

6
Application Events and Storage

In the previous chapter, we learned how to communicate with the backend database using a Cordova/PhoneGap app. However, even in an increasingly connected world, mobile devices aren't always connected to the network. As such, our app needs to be sensitive to changes in the device's network connectivity. It also needs to be sensitive to the type of network (for example, cellular versus wired), not to mention being sensitive to the device the app itself is running on.

Given all this, in this chapter, we'll cover the following topics:

- Determining network connectivity
- Getting the current network type
- Detecting changes in connectivity
- Handling connectivity issues
- Handling changes in the application state
- Responding to application-level events
- Storing local data using **SQLite**
- Storing data in the iOS **Keychain**

Getting ready

You'll need a Cordova project for this chapter. You're welcome to use our project in the code package for this book, or you can create one yourself. You'll need to add the appropriate platforms and plugins in order to create a valid project.

If you're creating the project based on the code package for this book, use the following code to create a new Cordova project:

```
cordova create ch6 com.example.ch6 TaskerCH6 --copy-from /path/to/code/
package/ch6
```

 If you're creating the project from scratch, leave off the --copy-from switch.

Next, add the following requisite platforms and plugins; we'll cover what the plugins do as we progress through the chapter:

```
# Add platforms - remove iOS if not on a Mac:
cordova platform add ios android
# The following plugin is one you're already familiar with; we
# used it in Chapter 5
cordova plugin add https://github.com/EddyVerbruggen/
SSLCertificateChecker-PhoneGap-Plugin.git
# Plugins used in this chapter
cordova plugin add org.apache.cordova.device
cordova plugin add org.apache.cordova.network-information
cordova plugin add com.photokandy.localstorage
cordova plugin add https://github.com/brodysoft/Cordova-SQLitePlugin
cordova plugin add com.shazron.cordova.plugin.keychainutil
```

Determining network connectivity

In a perfect world, we'd never have to worry if the device was connected to the Internet or not, and if our backend was reachable. Of course, we don't live in that world, so we need to respond appropriately when the device's network connectivity changes.

What's critical to remember is that having a network connection *in no way* determines the reachability of a host. That is to say, it's entirely possible for a device to be connected to a Wi-Fi network or a mobile hotspot and yet is unable to contact your servers. This can happen for several reasons (any of which can prevent proper communication with your backend).

In short, determining the network status and being sensitive to changes in the status really tells you only one thing: whether or not it is futile to attempt communication. After all, if the device isn't connected to any network, there's no reason to attempt communication over a nonexistent network. On the other hand, if a network is available, the only way to determine if your hosts are reachable or not is to *try and contact them*.

The ability to determine the device's network connectivity and respond to changes in the status is not available in Cordova/PhoneGap by default. You'll need to add a plugin before you can use this particular feature.

You can install the plugin as follows:

```
cordova plugin add org.apache.cordova.network-information
```

The plugin's complete documentation is available at: `https://github.com/apache/cordova-plugin-network-information/blob/master/doc/index.md`.

Getting the current network type

Anytime after the `deviceready` event fires, you can query the plugin for the status of the current network connection by querying `navigator.connection.type`:

```
var networkType = navigator.connection.type;
switch (networkType) {
  case Connection.UNKNOWN:
  console.log ("Unknown connection."); break;
  case Connection.ETHERNET:
  console.log ("Ethernet connection."); break;
  case Connection.WIFI:
  console.log ("Wi-Fi connection."); break;
  case Connection.CELL_2G:
  console.log ( "Cellular (2G) connection."); break;
  case Connection.CELL_3G:
  console.log ( "Cellular (3G) connection."); break;
  case Connection.CELL_4G:
  console.log ( "Cellular (4G) connection."); break;
```

```
    case Connection.CELL:
    console.log ( "Cellular connection."); break;
    case Connection.NONE:
    console.log ( "No network connection."); break;
}
```

If you executed the preceding code on a typical mobile device, you'd probably either see some variation of the `Cellular connection` or the `Wi-Fi connection` message. If your device was on Wi-Fi and you proceeded to disable it and rerun the app, the Wi-Fi notice will be replaced with the `Cellular connection` notice. Now, if you put the device into airplane mode and rerun the app, you should see **No network connection**.

Based on the available network type constants, it's clear that we can use this information in various ways:

- We can tell if it makes sense to attempt a network request: if the type is `Connection.NONE`, there's no point in trying as there's no network to service the request.

- We can tell if we are on a wired network, a Wi-Fi network, or a cellular network. Consider a streaming video app; this app can not only permit full quality video on a wired/Wi-Fi network, but can also use a lower quality video stream if it was running on a cellular connection.

Although tempting, there's one thing the earlier code *does not* tell us: the speed of the network. That is, we can't use the type of the network as a proxy for the available bandwidth, even though it feels like we can. After all, aren't Ethernet connections typically faster than Wi-Fi connections? Also, isn't a 4G cellular connection faster than a 2G connection?

In ideal circumstances, you'd be right. Unfortunately, it's possible for a fast 4G cellular network to be very congested, thus resulting in poor throughput. Likewise, it is possible for an Ethernet connection to communicate over a *noisy* wire and interact with a heavily congested network. This can also slow throughput.

Also, while it's important to recognize that although you can learn something about the network the device is connected to, you *can't* use this to learn anything about the network conditions beyond that network. The device might indicate that it is attached to a Wi-Fi network, but this Wi-Fi network might actually be a mobile hotspot. It could be connected to a satellite with high latency, or to a blazing fast fiber network.

As such, the only two things we can know for sure is whether or not it makes sense to attempt a request, and whether or not we need to limit the bandwidth if the device knows it is on a cellular connection. That's it. Any other use of this information is an abuse of the plugin, and is likely to cause undesirable behavior.

Detecting changes in connectivity

Determining the type of network connection once does little good as the device can lose the connection or join a new network at any time. This means that we need to properly respond to these events in order to provide a good user experience.

> Do not rely on the following events being fired when your app starts up for the first time. On some devices, it might take several seconds for the first event to fire; however, in some cases, the events might never fire (specifically, if testing in a simulator).

There are two events our app needs to listen to: the `online` event and the `offline` event. Their names are indicative of their function, so chances are good you already know what they do.

The `online` event is fired when the device connects to a network, assuming it wasn't connected to a network before. The `offline` event does the opposite: it is fired when the device loses a connection to a network, but only if the device was previously connected to a network. This means that you can't depend on these events to detect *changes* in the *type* of the network: a move from a Wi-Fi network to a cellular network might not elicit any events at all.

In order to listen to these events, you can use the following code:

```
document.addEventListener ("online", handleOnlineEvent, false);
document.addEventListener ("offline", handleOfflineEvent, false);
```

The event listener doesn't receive any information, so you'll almost certainly want to check the network type when handling an `online` event. The `offline` event will always correspond to a `Connection.NONE` network type.

Having the ability to detect changes in the connectivity status means that our app can be more intelligent about how it handles network requests, but it doesn't tell us if a request is guaranteed to succeed.

Handling connectivity issues

As the only way to know if a network request might succeed is to actually attempt the request, we need to know how to properly handle the errors that might rise out of such an attempt.

If you recall our promisified XHR wrapper from *Chapter 5, Communicating between Mobile and the Middle-Tier,* you should know that it can throw several different kinds of errors (defined at the top of /www/js/app/lib/xhr.js):

- `TimeoutError`: This error is thrown when the XHR times out. (Default is 30 seconds for our wrapper, but if the XHR's timeout isn't otherwise set, it will attempt to wait forever.)

- `HTTPError`: This error is thrown when the XHR completes and receives a response other than 200 OK. This can indicate any number of problems, but it *does not* indicate a network connectivity issue.

- `JSONError`: This error is thrown when the XHR completes, but the JSON response from the server cannot be parsed. Something is clearly wrong on the server, of course, but this *does not* indicate a connectivity issue.

- `XHRError`: This error is thrown when an error occurs when executing the XHR. This is definitely indicative of something going very wrong (not *necessarily* a connectivity issue, but there's a good chance).

- `MaxRetryAttemptsReached`: This error is thrown when the XHR wrapper has given up retrying the request. The wrapper automatically retries in the case of `TimeoutError` and `XHRError`.

In all the earlier cases, the catch method in the promise chain is called. At this point, you can attempt to determine the type of error in order to determine what to do next:

```
function sendFailRequest() {
  XHR.send( "GET", "http://www.really-bad-host-name.com
  /this/will/fail" )
  .then(function( response ) {
    console.log( response );
  })
  .catch( function( err ) {
    if ( err instanceof XHR.XHRError ||
    err instanceof XHR.TimeoutError ||
    err instanceof XHR.MaxRetryAttemptsReached ) {
      if ( navigator.connection.type === Connection.NONE ) {
        // we could try again once we have a network connection
        var retryRequest = function() {
          sendFailRequest();
```

```
            APP.removeGlobalEventListener( "networkOnline",
            retryRequest );
        };
        // wait for the network to come online - we'll cover
        this method in a moment
        APP.addGlobalEventListener( "networkOnline",
        retryRequest );
      } else {
        // we have a connection, but can't get through
        something's going on that we can't fix.
        alert( "Notice: can't connect to the server." );
      }
    }
    if ( err instanceof XHR.HTTPError ) {
      switch ( err.HTTPStatus ) {
        case 401: // unauthorized, log the user back in
        break;
        case 403: // forbidden, user doesn't have access
        break;
        case 404: // not found
        break;
        case 500: // internal server error
        break;
        default:
        console.log( "unhandled error: ", err.HTTPStatus );
      }
    }
    if ( err instanceof XHR.JSONParseError ) {
      console.log( "Issue parsing XHR response from server." );
    }
  }).done();
}
sendFailRequest();
```

Once a connection error is encountered, it's largely up to you and the type of app you are building to determine what to do next, but there are several options to consider as your next course of action:

- Fail loudly and let the user know that their last action failed. It might not be terribly great for user experience, but it might be the only sensible thing to do.

- Check whether there is a network connection present, and if not, hold on to the request until an online event is received and then send the request again. This makes sense only if the request you are sending is a request for data, not a request for changing data, as the data might have changed in the interim.

Handling changes in the application state

Your app almost certainly won't be the only app running on the user's mobile device. As such, the app needs to properly handle being *backgrounded* and then later being resumed by the operating system. The app should also have a strategy in place to deal with unexpected terminations as the operating system (or the user) might terminate any app at will.

The `pause` event is fired when the app is being placed in the background by the user or by the operating system. The `resume` event is fired when the user or the operating system brings the app back to the foreground. Note that there is *no* guarantee that your app will receive a `resume` event after a `pause` event; the operating system might terminate the app instead. In this case, the app will restart from the beginning with *no* `resume` event received.

The ideal situation is that the app will be paused for a short time and then resumed shortly thereafter. In this case, there's no need to worry about saving the app's state because the app was never terminated in the first place. Unfortunately, there is limited memory, so paused apps are prime targets for termination by the operating system, which means your app must be prepared for an unexpected termination.

For some apps, this might not be a big deal, especially if it's a read-only app with only a couple of views. On the other hand, for apps that deal with data entry, this can be a disaster as it can result in the loss of the last entry the individual was working on.

As a result, apps should *at minimum* work to prevent data loss after a `pause` event. However, most apps try to go further: they attempt to appear as if the app was *never terminated* at all. This means tracking the state of every view, the position in any scrollable areas, the text in any fields, and restoring the entire session when the application is restarted. Although slick, it's also a difficult task to accomplish for many apps, so most apps will live somewhere in the middle; let's try not to lose any data, and let's restore to a state that allows the user to quickly get back to work.

None of this is to say that the app can't be terminated at other times, either due to a crash or user intervention. To reduce data loss in these scenarios, apps will often save data to a local store on a periodic basis or when the data is entered or modified. This works as long as the app can save the data quickly without slowing down the user interface. Other apps simply take the approach that if the app is terminated unexpectedly in this manner, then the data loss here is acceptable. It's entirely possible that some bug in the app *caused* a crash, and given the same data, the app can enter an endless crash cycle.

Listening to these events is very similar to listening to the `online` or `offline` events; the following shows the code for listening for an app pausing and resuming:

```
document.addEventListener ("pause", appIsPausing, false);
document.addEventListener ("resume", appIsResuming, false);
```

There's one problem that Cordova/PhoneGap throws into the mix when targeting iOS: during the `pause` event, no *native code* or *plugin* can execute. Whereas, on other platforms, this issue is not present. Therefore, one can choose to save state to a file on the device's persistent storage via the File API, and so on. However, in iOS, this is *not* an option.

You might think then that it would be safe to persist data to local storage when running on iOS, and you'd be right, as long as you had already saved the data (via polling or on a data change). If, on the other hand, you save the data during the `pause` event, and the app is terminated after being backgrounded, local storage itself is *not* saved. (For more information, see `https://github.com/photokandyStudios/ PKLocalStorage`).

To rectify this problem in iOS, you either need to make sure that the data has been saved well in advance of the app ever being backgrounded, or you'll need to add two additional plugins. One is a core plugin that enables us to detect the device platform aptly called `device` (`org.apache.cordova.device`). We need this so that the app can decide how to act based on the platform it is running on. You can install the plugin as follows:

`cordova plugin add org.apache.cordova.device`

The other is a custom plugin I wrote called `PKLocalStorage` (`com.photokandy. localstorage`). Use the following command to install it:

`cordova plugin add com.photokandy.localstorage`

This plugin does most of its work automatically: it ensures that local storage is persisted even after an app termination. However, in order to do so, one needs to respond to events slightly differently on iOS than on other platforms:

```
if ( device.platform === "iOS" ) {
  // if we want to persist changes to localStorage during
  // a pause event, we need to use the PKLocalStorage plugin
  window.PKLocalStorage.addPauseHandler( appIsPausing );
  window.PKLocalStorage.addResumeHandler( appIsResuming );
} else {
  document.addEventListener ("pause", appIsPausing, false);
  document.addEventListener ("resume", appIsResuming, false);
}
```

The reason why different code is needed is because the PKLocalStorage plugin needs to know when it can safely save the contents of local storage. The only time it is safe to write to local storage during a backgrounding event is when a handler is called from the plugin via addPauseHandler.

Responding to application-level events

Although you can have the code that responds to events in the same handler, it's often better to have this code localized to the files (simply for readability and understandability). This means that the event handlers we've discussed so far simply become dispatchers on receipt of an event; they might notify any number of methods in the app when the event occurs.

A lot of JavaScript and UI frameworks have built-in methods to support this event notification system, but here we'll be generic. Such a system needs three methods: a method to register a listener for an event, a method to remove the listener, and a method to dispatch the event to all the listeners. We can define these methods in www/js/app/main.js.

First, let's define an object to hold our events and listeners, and then define addGlobalEventListener:

```
var globalEventListeners = {};
APP.addGlobalEventListener = function
addGlobalEventListener( event, listener ) {
  var EVENT = event.toUpperCase();
  if ( typeof globalEventListeners[ EVENT ] === "undefined" ) {
    globalEventListeners[ EVENT ] = [];
  }
  globalEventListeners[ EVENT ].push( listener );
};
```

Next, we need a way to remove listeners when they aren't needed anymore:

```
APP.removeGlobalEventListener = function
removeGlobalEventListener( event, listener ) {
  var EVENT = event.toUpperCase();
  var i = -1;
  if ( typeof globalEventListeners[ EVENT ] !== "undefined" ) {
    i = globalEventListeners[ EVENT ].indexOf( listener );
    if ( i > -1 ) {
      globalEventListeners[ EVENT ].splice( i, 1 );
    }
  }
};
```

Now, we need to define the method that dispatches the events:

```
APP.dispatchGlobalEvent =
function dispatchGlobalEvent( event, sync ) {
  var EVENT = event.toUpperCase();
  var doSynchronously = false;
  if ( typeof sync !== "undefined" ) {
    doSynchronously = sync;
  }
  if ( typeof globalEventListeners[ EVENT ] !== "undefined" ) {
    globalEventListeners[ EVENT ].forEach( function
    dispatchToListener( listener ) {
      if ( doSynchronously ) {
        try {
          listener( EVENT );
        } catch ( err ) {
          console.log( "dispatchGlobalEvent caught error: " +
          JSON.stringify( err ) );
        }
      } else {
        setTimeout( function asyncDispatch() {
          listener( EVENT );
        }, 0 );
      }
    });
  }
};
```

All the previously shown method does is loop through every registered listener for a given event and then call the listener. If `sync` is `true`, the listeners are called synchronously, which is important for any events responding to a `pause` event (if they execute asynchronously, they might not execute before the app gets backgrounded). If `sync` is `false`, the listeners are called asynchronously.

Now, we can register listeners at any point in our app and react accordingly:

```
function saveDataBeforePause() {
  localStorage.pauseInProgress = "true";
  localStorage.dataToSave = JSON.stringify( {
    "name": "Bob Smith","manager": "John Doe"
  });
}
APP.addGlobalEventListener( "applicationPausing",
saveDataBeforePause );
function cleanUpAfterResume() {
```

```
        localStorage.removeItem( "pauseInProgress" );
        localStorage.removeItem( "dataToSave" );
    }
    APP.addGlobalEventListener( "applicationResuming",
    cleanUpAfterResume );
    // check if we have data to restore at app start
    if ( typeof localStorage.pauseInProgress !== "undefined" ) {
        var savedData = JSON.parse( localStorage.dataToSave );
        console.log( savedData );
        cleanUpAfterResume();
    }
```

 Local storage is not stored with any encryption. If an attacker can unlock your device and plug it in to a computer, they can access the contents of local storage. As such, *do not* store anything sensitive to local storage during `pause` events.

The preceding code will save some data when the application is put in the background. This also saves a variable that it can check when the app is started or resumed in order to determine if there is data that should be restored. When the application is resumed with no intervening termination, the data in local storage is simply removed as there's no need to keep it, since the app hasn't been terminated. If the application is terminated and then resumed, the code checks for the existence of `pauseInProgress`, and if it exists, it retrieves the data and removes it from local storage.

Storing local data using SQLite

Most apps can get by with storing data using local storage or the **File** API. However, sometimes data needs to be stored locally in a relational method, and SQLite allows you to do just that. There was a standard for HTML5 that used SQLite behind the scenes, but this is now deprecated. This was also limited to five megabytes of data. The SQLite plugin, on the other hand, is not limited by size constraints other than the space available on the device. If you are familiar with the HTML5's **Web SQL** API, the SQLite API is very similar.

The SQLite plugin we're using doesn't live in the Cordova plugin registry, so it must be added via URL. When adding the plugin, use `https://github.com/brodysoft/Cordova-SQLitePlugin` instead of the following plugin ID:

```
cordova plugin add https://github.com/brodysoft/Cordova-SQLitePlugin
```

To open or create a database, you can use the following at any time after `deviceready` has been fired:

```
var db = window.sqlitePlugin.openDatabase
( {name: "datastore.db"} );
```

Once created, you can create a transaction and then issue SQL queries:

```
db.transaction ( function (tx) {
  tx.executeSql ("CREATE TABLE IF NOT EXISTS our_table
  ( id integer primary key, data text )");
  tx.executeSql ("INSERT INTO our_table (data) VALUES (?)",
  ["some data"], function (tx, res) {
    tx.executeSql ( "SELECT id, data FROM our_table", [],
    function (tx, res) {
      console.log (res.rows.length);
      console.log (res.rows.item(0).id);
      console.log (res.rows.item(0).data);
    });
  });
}, function (err) {
  console.log (err.message);
});
```

As with local storage and data stored using the File API, the data is easily readable by anyone who has access to the device. SQLite does offer the option to encrypt the database using **SQLCipher**, and if you need it, you can follow these links for the installation:

- For Android: `http://brodyspark.blogspot.com/2012/12/using-sqlcipher-for-android-with.html`, `http://brodyspark.blogspot.com/2012/12/enhancements-to-sqlcipher-db-classes.html`

- For iOS: `http://brodyspark.blogspot.com/2012/12/integrating-sqlcipher-with.html`

Using SQLCipher (http://sqlcipher.net) does require that the database should have a secret key. Although the examples in the previous posts include the secret in the code itself, you should *never* store the password in *your* code. Typically, the secret will be obtained from the user (perhaps, a combination of their username and password) or from the server. If the secret is apt to change, you will need to first open the database using the old secret and rekey the database using the new secret:

```
var db = window.sqlitePlugin.openDatabase(
{name: "datastore.db", key: oldSecret } );
db.transaction ( function (tx) {
  tx.executeSql ( "PRAGMA rekey = ?", [ newSecret ] )
});
```

As with all things in SQL, you do need to be very careful with SQL injection. In the previously shown examples, we've been using bind variables. The question marks are placeholders. Each placeholder corresponds to the same index in the second array that we've passed to executeSQL. That is, the first placeholder corresponds to the first item in the array, and so on.

You should *never* do the following as it is extremely susceptible to SQL injection:

```
tx.executeSql ( "SELECT * FROM our_table WHERE id=" + desiredId );
```

All an attacker has to do is get desiredId to have some malicious SQL in it, and you've lost the entire database. To be sure, it's local, but it can still have huge ramifications for your app.

Unfortunately, going over SQL and SQLite in full is beyond the scope of this book. We suggest looking at SQLite's homepage (http://www.sqlite.org) and reviewing the documentation available there.

Storing data in the iOS Keychain

When it comes to storing data securely, the best method is to use something made for secure storage. In iOS, this is the Keychain. In Android, there is a Keychain of sorts, but it's not a general data store as is the iOS Keychain. As such, this section is for iOS only. For Android, the best place to store secure data is in the application's data directory on internal storage. It's not a complete protection, but neither is the iOS Keychain. (Should the device be rooted, all bets are off as the data is easily accessible. This applies to both iOS and Android.)

For more information regarding the Keychain itself, see: https://developer. apple.com/library/mac/documentation/Security/Conceptual/ keychainServConcepts/02concepts/concepts.html.

First, you need to install the plugin:

```
cordova plugin add com.shazron.cordova.plugin.keychainutil
```

Next, you might want to read up on the entire documentation available at: http://plugins.cordova.io/#/package/com.shazron.cordova.plugin.keychainutil. We'll take what is discussed there, promisify it, and then store some data in the Keychain for safekeeping, but first, one needs to create a new Keychain instance:

```
var kc = new Keychain();
```

Then, one can use setForKey (success, failure, key, service, value) to store a value, or getForKey (success, failure, key, service) in order to retrieve a value. removeForKey (success, failure, key, service) will delete an item.

The callback structure of these functions is a bit painful; however, it is easier to promisfy them:

```
var setKeyInKeyChain = function( keychain, key, service, value ) {
  var deferred = Q.defer();
  keychain.setForKey( function() {
    deferred.resolve();
  }, function() {
    deferred.reject();
  }, key, service, value );
  return deferred.promise;
};
var getKeyInKeyChain = function( keychain, key, service ) {
  var deferred = Q.defer();
  keychain.getForKey( function( v ) {
    deferred.resolve( v );
  }, function() {
    deferred.reject();
  }, key, service );
  return deferred.promise;
};
```

Now that we've defined these functions, we can store and retrieve data, as shown in the following code:

```
setKeyInKeyChain( kc, "secretData", "security",
JSON.stringify( dataToStore ) ).then(function() {
  return getKeyInKeyChain( kc, "secretData", "security" );
}).then( function( v ) {
  console.log( v );
```

```
}).catch( function( err ) {
  console.log( err );
} ).done();
```

 The documentation for this plugin indicates that JSON data needs to be escaped, though we didn't find that to be the case. Nevertheless, if you have problems retrieving JSON data from the Keychain, you might wish to review the documentation and escape the data being stored to the Keychain.

Summary

We've covered quite a bit in this chapter. We've dealt with handling different network connection types, how to respond to online and offline events, and how to respond to backgrounding and resumption of the app by the user or the operating system. Finally, we briefly covered how to use SQLite to store local data. We also covered how to use the iOS Keychain to store secure data.

In the next chapter we'll cover how to send and receive push notifications to iOS and Android. After that, we'll finally be ready to put everything together into a real, live app in the final chapter.

7
Push Notifications

Apps that rely on dynamic content often need a way to alert the users of the app that existing content has changed or if new content is available. Although it is possible for an app to repeatedly poll a server for changes or to create a web socket so that changes can be sent in real time from the server, neither option works when the app is in the background. Furthermore, polling is bad for battery life. Push Notifications come to the rescue; these are OS-level services that can display notifications even when our app isn't running, and they can do so in a way that doesn't drain batteries as much as continuous polling. Most platforms also provide some degree of fault tolerance: if the device isn't able to receive a Push Notification, the last notice is usually stored in the cloud until the device is in a situation where it can receive the notice.

In this chapter we'll cover the following topics:

- Push Notification architecture
- Boxcar Universal Push Notifications platform
- Integrate Boxcar into PhoneGap/Cordova
- Send Push via Boxcar
- Receive Pushes from Boxcar

Delving into Push Notification architecture

Push Notifications are an implementation of the publish/subscribe pattern. Clients (mobile devices) can subscribe to a specific channel, and data can be published in these channels from the backend infrastructure. Often, the request is regarding a specific piece of data, but it's also possible to publish more general data, such as a notification that all users of the system need to see.

Typically, Push Notification architectures look something like the following figure:

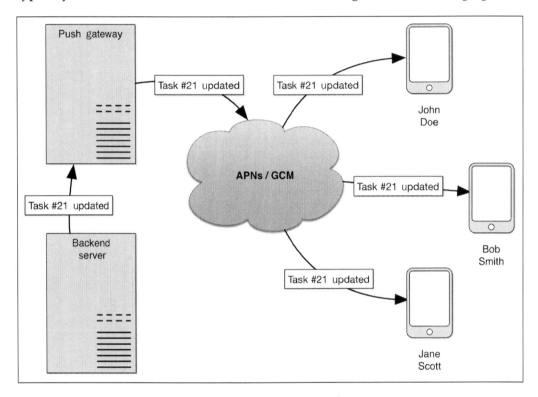

Push Notifications originate from the backend (although pushes can be generated from clients as well), and these notifications are often routed through a gateway that forwards the notification to the appropriate provider (Apple or Google). The gateway can be a service running on a local server in your data center, or it can be a service provided by a third party. In our case, we'll use a service named Boxcar (http://www.boxcar.io), but there are many other options available, including Parse (http://www.parse.com) and push-notify (https://www.npmjs.org/package/push-notify).

Technically, a gateway isn't required; the Push Notification package mentioned earlier will function just fine if it was included directly within our Node.js server application. The benefit of having a gateway, on the other hand, is that it can take care of the platform-specific implementation of Push Notifications, and anything that needs to send a Push Notification in our app (or even the enterprise) only needs to send a request to the gateway.

 It is important to recognize that there is *no* guarantee that the clients will receive any Push Notifications that are sent. Your app should be able to work properly *without* push; push should only augment the app's experience.

Boxcar Universal Push Notifications Platform

While it's entirely possible to rely only on internal software for Push Notifications, it does simplify development by utilizing a third-party Push Notification gateway service. We've chosen Boxcar for our demo app not only because it's fast and scalable, but also because it offers an HTTP API that allows us to generate pushes from anything capable of generating an HTTP request (which includes JavaScript, Node.js, and our Oracle database server). Boxcar also provides a **PhoneGap SDK** that is easy to embed without having to worry about a lot of platform-specific code. Finally, Boxcar also provides a free service tier of up to 200 pushes per minute and a device limit of 100 Android devices and iOS devices. After these limits are reached, the price for the service is based solely on the number of pushes sent per minute. The following steps show how to sign up and begin with your project:

1. Sign up at `https://console.boxcar.io/users/sign_up`. You can peruse the available content and price tiers at `https://www.boxcar.io/developer`.

2. Once you've got an account, you need to create a new project:

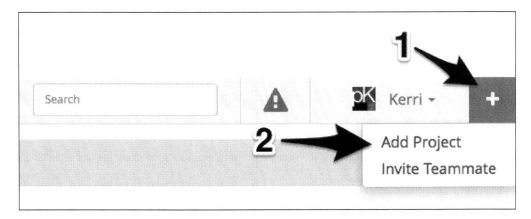

3. At this point, you'll be asked for a project name as well as an optional icon:

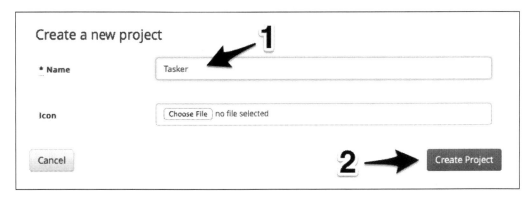

After you create a project, you'll be presented with a dashboard that allows you to set up notifications for each platform you want to target. Boxcar supports several platforms, but for our purposes, we'll only worry about iOS and Android.

Setting up Apple Push Notifications with Boxcar

In order to set up Apple Push Notifications, click on the **Apple** logo below the **Devices Configuration** heading.

The Apple Push Notification service has the concept of a development and production environment. The certificates and configuration for the development environment are different from the production environment. Therefore, in the following steps, we've highlighted where you'll need to repeat steps when moving your app into production.

Perform the following steps:

1. Under **Apple Push Certificates**, click on **Create Your SSL Certificate?** You'll want to use the button in the development row for now, but when you move to production, you'll need to repeat these steps for the production row.

If you already have a certificate previously generated, you can upload it to Boxcar instead.

2. A new dialog box will appear; click on **Download a CSR file** to download a certificate request that you will send to Apple.

3. After the CSR is downloaded, click on the **Apple** link in the dialog box, or navigate to `https://developer.apple.com/account/overview.action` and click on **Identifiers**. It's best to do this in a new browser tab.

4. Click on **App IDs** to display the application identifiers associated with your account.

5. Click on the **+** icon to add a new app ID.

6. Assign a human-readable name to the ID; we used **Tasker PGE CH7** for this chapter.

7. Make sure that **Explicit App ID** is selected (it should be selected by default).

8. Enter a unique reverse domain application ID in the **Bundle ID** field; you should use the same ID you specified when creating your Cordova/PhoneGap app. We used `com.packtpub.pgech7` for this chapter.

9. Scroll down to **App Services** and check **Data Protection** (make sure **Complete** is marked) and **Push Notifications**.

10. Click on **Continue**, and when the next screen appears, click on **Submit** after you've reviewed everything is correct.

11. Click on **App IDs** in the sidebar again and click on your new application ID. The row should expand with all the services associated with the app ID; there should be an **Edit** button near the bottom of this row, click on it.

12. Under the Push Notifications section, click on **Create Certificate…**; be sure to use the same section as you used in step one (**development/production**).

13. A new dialog box will appear (indicating that you need to create a CSR). Boxcar has already done this for us, so just click on **Continue**.

14. Select **Choose File…** and locate the CSR you downloaded from Boxcar and click on **Choose/OK**.

15. Once the file has been uploaded, click on **Generate** to create the actual certificate.

16. Wait a few seconds. When **Your Certificate is Ready** appears, click on the **Download** button to download the certificate to your computer.

17. Return to Boxcar's browser tab and click on **Step 2, Upload the CER file**.

18. Upload the certificate you downloaded from Apple.

19. You should receive an email indicating that Boxcar attempted to connect to Apple using the certificate provided and that the attempt was successful.

20. Make a note of the **Access Key** and **Secret Key** in this page; you'll need it so that iOS devices can receive Push Notifications.

Setting up Google Cloud Messages with Boxcar

In order to target Android, you'll need to click on the **Android** icon on the project's settings page and perform the following steps:

1. In a new tab, open your Google Developer's Console (`https://console.developers.google.com`) and sign in using your Google Developer credentials. (If you don't have an account, you'll need to create one.)

2. Click on the **Create Project** button.

3. In the new dialog, enter the project's name and ID. The ID is not something you can change later, so double check that you've entered it correctly. For our sample, we used `Tasker CH7` as the name and `taskerch7` as the project ID.

4. Read the Google Cloud Platform terms of service and then check the appropriate box to indicate your agreement.

5. Click on **Create**.

6. Next, click on **Enable an API** on the resulting dashboard.

7. Scroll down to **Google Cloud Messaging for Android** and click on the **OFF** button (this will enable the service).

8. A new dialog box will appear. Read the terms of service and check the appropriate box and click on **Accept**.

9. In the sidebar, click on **Credentials**. Then, click on **Create New Key**.

10. Click on **Server key** in the resulting dialog box.

11. If you want, you can limit what servers can send notifications by entering their IP addresses in the **Accept Requests From These Server IP Addresses** box. If you don't want to limit who can send notifications, leave this blank.

12. Click on **Create**.

13. An **API KEY** will appear; copy this to your clipboard.

14. Return to the Boxcar browser tab.

15. Under the **Android Push Credentials** heading, paste the key you just copied in the **API Key** field.

16. Click on **Update Client**.

17. Make a note of the Access Key and Secret Key from this page; you'll need them so that Android devices can receive Push Notifications.

18. Return to your Google Developer's Console and return to your project's overview page.

19. Take note of the **Project ID** as you'll need this number later.

Downloading the Boxcar PhoneGap SDK

Now that you've configured Boxcar, you should download the SDK for PhoneGap/Cordova. At the bottom of your Boxcar dashboard, there should be an **SDK & Docs** link, click on it. A new screen will appear with several SDKs, as shown in the following screenshot. Click on the download button in the PhoneGap section:

Integrating Boxcar with PhoneGap/Cordova

At this point, we can create a PhoneGap/Cordova project and integrate it with Boxcar. We've got a sample project at /ch7 in the code package; all it does is respond to Push Notifications by displaying an alert. You're welcome to use our code as a base, or perform the following steps to integrate Boxcar with your app:

1. Create your project using the Cordova CLI as normal (however, use the app ID you used when setting up Push Notifications):

    ```
    cordova create ./ch7 com.packtpub.pgech7 TaskerCH7
    ```

2. Add the iOS and Android platforms:

    ```
    cordova platform add ios android
    ```

3. Add the necessary plugins; Boxcar requires the following two plugins:

    ```
    cordova plugin add org.apache.cordova.device
    cordova plugin add https://github.com/boxcar/PushPlugin
    ```

4. Copy the Boxcar.js file from the Boxcar SDK and place it in your project's www directory.

> We had to make several changes to the Boxcar.js file in order to function as needed for our purposes. We've submitted these features and bug fixes to Boxcar, but if they haven't updated their SDK to support these changes, you might want to utilize our custom copy of Boxcar.js in the /boxcar folder in the code package for this book.

5. Load the Boxcar.js file and the PushNotification.js file using script tags in your index.html file:

    ```
    <script type="text/javascript" src="PushNotification.js">
    <script type="text/javascript" src="Boxcar.js">
    ```

> If you're paying attention to your directory structure, you might wonder where PushNotification.js is coming from; it's installed by the PushPlugin we added in step three, but it resides in the root directory of your platform-specific www directory. This only occurs when the project is prepared or built, so it's not immediately apparent where this file lives. In your code, you can just assume it's in the root directory where your index.html file lives.

The preceding code works well if you aren't using **RequireJS** or another module loader. If you are, however, you might want to place Boxcar.js in a library folder within your directory structure and then configure your module loader appropriately. For example, since our demo uses RequireJS, we placed Boxcar.js in /www/js/app/lib/Boxcar.js and used the following configuration in www/js/app.js:

```
requirejs.config( {
  baseUrl: './js/lib',
  paths: { …
    'Boxcar': '../app/lib/Boxcar',
    'PushNotifications': '../../PushNotification'
  },
  shim: { …
    "PushNotifications": {
      exports: "PushNotification"
    },
    "Boxcar": {
      exports: "Boxcar",
      deps: [ "PushNotifications" ]
    }
  }
} );
```

At this point, you can begin to write code that uses Boxcar to listen to Push Notifications. However, before you can do so, you need to initialize Boxcar with your Access Keys and Secret Keys (this must be done after deviceready has been fired):

```
APIKeys = {
  ios: {
    clientKey: "Access Key obtained from Boxcar for iOS client",
    secret: "Secret obtained from Boxcar for iOS client"
  },
  android: {
    clientKey: "Access Key obtained from Boxcar for Android",
    secret: "Secret obtained from Boxcar for Android client",
    androidSenderID: "Project ID obtained from Google"
  }
};
Boxcar.init( {
  server: "https://boxcar-api.io",
  richUrlBase: "https://boxcar-push.s3.amazonaws.com",
  ios: APIKeys.ios,
  android: APIKeys.android
} );
```

Once `init` has been called, you're ready to start listening to Push Notifications, but you need to perform a couple of configuration steps first for each platform.

Additional iOS configuration steps

Before your app will respond to Push Notifications, you need to download the appropriate entitlements from Apple. To do this, follow these steps:

1. Launch **Xcode** and open the project we just created (the Xcode project will be located under `/platforms/ios` with a `.xcodeproj` extension).

2. Open the Xcode menu and click on **Preferences**.

3. Click on the **Accounts** tab.

4. Next, click on your Apple Developer account if it isn't already selected. Then, click on **View Details...**

5. Click on the refresh icon in the lower-left corner of the dialog box and wait for a few seconds while Xcode downloads your entitlements. When done, you should have a new entitlement for Push Notifications.

6. Now that you've downloaded your entitlements, exit out of the dialog box and then build your project once. Although it won't work yet, doing this now will ensure that you can utilize the Cordova CLI to build and deploy this project in the future rather than using Xcode.

Additional Android Configuration steps

According to Boxcar's SDK documentation, you also need to add an entry to the `/platforms/android/res/xml/config.xml` file after adding the plugin using the Cordova CLI. Find the `<widget>` element and add the following code:

```
<plugin name="Storage" value="org.apache.cordova.Storage" />
```

Receiving Pushes from Boxcar

Although it might seem counterintuitive to work on the code that listens to Push Notifications before we work on the code to send them, it's really not. Boxcar allows you to send any number of pushes from their dashboard, which means that we can initially focus on receiving pushes before we worry about how to send them.

In order to receive pushes, our app needs to register the device with Boxcar. When we register our device, we can specify what kind of Push Notifications we are interested in using **tags**. Tags enable us to target pushes to specific consumers without the need to know the specific device information (such as their UUID). Tags are akin to channels, if that helps.

Our demo app just registers for two specific tags, but when we put everything together in the next chapter, we'll actually listen using a tag based on the authenticated user's username. This will enable our backend to send a Push Notification to a username, and it will reach them on any of the devices they have logged in on.

 If the app subscribes to a tag that doesn't exist, Boxcar will create the tag for us. There is a mechanism in the Boxcar console that allows you to create tags ahead of time, if you so choose, but this isn't required.

Along with the tags we're interested in, we also send along some device information in our demo app: the device's unique identifier and an alias. This alias can be anything we want; when we put everything together, it will look like BSMITH iPad 3,1 iOS 7.1, which is easy for humans to read, so even though the alias is optional, it's better to send it. The unique identifier is actually not required by Boxcar. You can send it, if you like, but it is completely optional. It's also important to recognize that this unique identifier might not actually be something that can identify the device, but only be unique to the app. For more information regarding the UUID in Cordova, see https://github.com/apache/cordova-plugin-device/blob/master/doc/index.md#deviceuuid).

Here's what our demo code looks like:

```
Boxcar.registerDevice( {
    mode: "development",    // or production
    onsuccess: notificationSuccess.bind( undefined,
    "Device Registered" ),
    onerror: notificationError,
    onalert: notificationReceived,
    onnotificationclick: notificationClicked,
    udid: device.uuid, // optional
    alias: [ "BSMITH", device.platform, device.model,
    device.version ].join(" "), // optional
    tags: [ "_general", "BSMITH" ]
} );
```

When the device is successfully registered, the onsuccess handler will be called. In our case, it's a partially applied function designed to write **Device Registered** to the console and alert this to the user as well:

```
function notificationSuccess( msgToLog ) {
  console.log( msgToLog );
  alert( msgToLog );
}
```

If an error occurs during registration, the onerror handler is called instead. Again, in our demo, it logs the error to the console and alerts the user, but in a real application, you can take additional steps in an attempt to resolve the problem:

```
function notificationError( err ) {
  console.log( JSON.stringify( err ) );
  alert( JSON.stringify( err ) );
}
```

When a notification is received, the onalert handler will be called. If the user interacted with the notification as displayed by the operating system (while the app wasn't running or was backgrounded), the onnotificationclick handler will also be called.

The data sent to the handler is an object that includes the following properties:

- id: This is the unique identifier of the notification
- time: This is the the time when the notification was received
- sound: This is the sound that should be played when the notification is received
- badge: This is the number of unread messages (matters only for iOS)
- richPush: This indicates whether the Push Notification includes rich content
- url: This is an optional URL for the notification
- seen: This indicates whether the notification has been marked as received
- json: This is the complete notification data; use JSON.parse to convert it to a proper JSON object so that you can access any custom properties (such as a task ID)

Our demo handler doesn't do anything special with the incoming data other than to write it to the console and alert the user, but it does notify Boxcar that the message has been seen. It also resets the badge count (for iOS, this will also remove the notifications from the notification center as well):

```
function notificationReceived( data ) {
    console.log( JSON.stringify( data ) );
    alert( JSON.stringify( data ) );
    // indicate that we've seen the alert
    Boxcar.markAsReceived( {
        onsuccess: notificationSuccess.bind( undefined,
        "Notification marked as seen." ),
        onerror: notificationError,
        id: data.id
    } );
    Boxcar.resetBadge( {
        onsuccess: notificationSuccess.bind( undefined, "Badge
        reset." ),
        onerror: notificationError
    } );
}
```

markAsReceived should always be called to let Boxcar know that we've seen the notification. We also send a resetBadge request so that the badge on iOS is cleared (otherwise it will simply increase until we reset it later). It depends on the nature of your app whether you will want to call resetBadge at any other time.

The onnotificationclick handler simply alerts the user that the notification was clicked; this only occurs on Android, and although the handler is required, chances are good that you won't worry much about any code in this handler for typical Push Notifications.

Whenever the user is about to log out, you should unregister the device so that the device no longer receives notifications. This can be done, as shown in the following code:

```
Boxcar.unregisterDevice ({
    onsuccess: notificationSuccess.bind( undefined,
    "Device unregistered" ),onerror: notificationError
});
```

Normally, you wouldn't notify the user of this action, but it is useful to do so during debugging.

Background vs foreground Push Notifications

When the device receives a Push Notification, it first checks to see whether your app is in the foreground. If it is, the notification is passed directly to the app for display and handling. If the app isn't running or isn't in the foreground, the operating system displays the text of the Push Notification to the user. If the user interacts with the Push Notification, your app is launched (or resumed) and receives the same data so that it can handle the notification appropriately. In our demo app, the notification is redisplayed, but in the final app, we'll use the onnotificationclick handler to automatically navigate to the appropriate task (based on the Push Notification received).

If you need to determine whether the Push Notification was received while the app was in the foreground, you can use the json field of the incoming data object to do so:

```
var notification = JSON.parse(data);
if (notification.foreground) { // our app was in the foreground }
else { // our app wasn't in the foreground }
```

Sending a Push via Boxcar

Sending a Push Notification can be done quite easily from the Boxcar console, but this isn't useful when we want these pushes to be sent automatically. Thankfully, Boxcar utilizes an HTTP API, which means we can generate a push from anything that can generate HTTP requests.

You'll need to obtain the **Publisher Access Key** and **Publisher Secret Key** to send a Push Notification programmatically. To do this, follow these steps:

1. On the **Dashboard**, click on the gear icon for our Boxcar project.
2. Click on **Publishers**.
3. Click on **Tasker API** and you should be presented with a screen that contains the necessary keys as well as some example codes you can use. We have modified the Python example and placed it in /ch7/sendPush.

Sending a push boils down to this process:

1. A push object is created, as follows:

```
push = { "taskId": "21" , // custom data
  "f": "0",          // indicates if has rich content 0=no
  "i": "17327",      // id for push
  "badge": "auto", // badge (iOS) "auto" or a number
  "sound": "1.caf",// sound to play (optional)
  "priority": "normal", // priority
  "aps" : {
    "alert" : "Hello World!" // text to display
  },
  "expires" : 1409525432, // optional epoch time when the
  push expires
  "tags" : ["_general"] // tag/channel to target
}
```

2. The object is converted to a string.

3. A signature is computed based on the following input:

```
POST
boxcar-api.io
/api/push
<string representation of push object>
```

4. The signature is an SHA1 hash using the **Publisher Secret Key** as provided by Boxcar.

5. A URL request is formed like the following code (which includes all the properties from the preceding object):

```
https://boxcar-api.io/api/push/?publishkey=ACCESS_KEY
&signature=COMPUTED_SIGNATURE&taskId=21&f=0&i=17327&...
```

6. The request is sent. A very basic `curl` request is shown:

```
curl 'https://boxcarapi.io/api/push?publishkey=
ACCESS_KEY&signature=dc1e7dda93861b372c67c92f0b76bfb739988d
c0' -H Content-Type:application/json -d
'{"id":"111","aps":{"alert":"Hello
world!"},"expires":1409525432,"tags":["@all"]}'
```

Keep your **Publisher Access Key** and **Publisher Secret key** a *secret*! The only keys that should be present in the code that runs on your user devices should be the iOS and Android client keys and not the publisher keys. If these keys aren't kept secret, *anyone* can send messages to your app, not just you.

In our final app, sending this Push Notification will actually occur from the Oracle database server using **PL/SQL** to send the HTTP request. You can, however, send push notifications from Node.js, Python, or any other platform that supports sending HTTP requests.

Summary

We've covered quite a bit in this chapter. We discussed the typical architecture for Push Notifications and gateways, and we covered how to set up Push Notifications, using Boxcar, Apple, and Google Cloud Messaging. We also wrote code to send and receive Push Notifications.

In the next chapter, we will put everything together from the last several chapters to create one proper application that your users might actually want to use. We'll cover various presentation techniques (charts, templates, and so on) and frameworks, as well as how to wire everything together (models, view controllers, routes, and so on).

8
Building the Presentation Tier

Presentation is critical to any mobile application. Although the data tier, web services, and API are important, without the presentation tier, there's no way for the user to interact with your service.

This much is obvious, of course, but it's also important to plan your presentation as well. Users appreciate functional apps, but they also appreciate apps that are well designed and even beautiful. Enterprise apps might not always fall into the *beautiful* category, especially if there's a lot of data entry, but a well designed app that guides the user in their interactions is something that should be desired.

There's no possible way we can cover every possible presentation technique in this chapter, or even in this book; there are volumes dedicated solely to this part of app development alone. Having said that, we'll touch lightly on some of these basic concepts:

- Mock-up design tools
- Libraries and frameworks
- Common patterns (**MVC**, publish/subscribe, observables, templates, data binding, URL routing)
- Presentation (UI frameworks, View Management)
- Forms and validation
- Data visualization

Mock-up design tools

Although not required, it's a good idea to mock up your presentation tier so that you have a good idea of what will be required in order to implement it. There are many good mock-up tools available, and though some may not seem to be relevant to PhoneGap/Cordova, they are still incredibly useful. For example, the following is the mock-up that was created for the demo app using **OmniGraffle**:

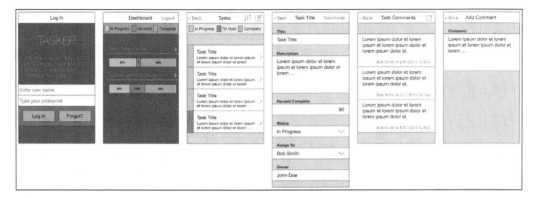

The following tools are incredibly useful when it comes to building mock-ups:

- **Proto.io** (http://proto.io, limited free plan available): This is an advanced prototyping for mobile devices. It allows preview on physical devices.

- **Moqups** (https://moqups.com, free plan available): This is an HTML5 app used for mobile wireframing.

- **Wireframe.cc** (https://wireframe.cc, free plan limited): This is a basic wireframing for HTML5 or mobile.

- **iPlotz** (http://iplotz.com): This provides mock-ups for the Web, desktop applications, and mobile devices. Free version is available.

- **Balsamiq** (http://balsamiq.com, $79): This app/web app supports web and mobile UI wireframe stencils. It also supports versioning your mock-ups.

- **FluidUI** (https://www.fluidui.com, free plan available): This is a software that provides on-device previews, low and high-fidelity stencils, sharing mock-ups with collaborators.

- **Omnigraffle** (http://www.omnigroup.com/omnigraffle/, $99, OSX and iPad): This is a diagramming tool with multiple stencils that supports mobile and web mock-ups.

Some UI frameworks also provide designer tools that are made to work with that particular framework (for example, Ionic Framework has such a tool in beta). These can be useful even if you aren't planning on using that particular framework.

Libraries and frameworks

The rest of this chapter will make more sense if we get some terminology straight. Cordova/PhoneGap apps will often make use of multiple utility libraries and usually one **User Interface** (**UI**) framework, though some frameworks also tend to blur the line between the two distinctions (I'll refer to these as mixed frameworks).

Utility libraries are intended to provide one or more features that make coding hybrid apps easier (things like object models, **MVC/MVVM** classes, templating functions, data binding features, and so on). Some utility libraries focus on providing one feature, while others package these features together. Most are typically quite small and aren't terribly opinionated.

Utility frameworks, on the other hand, provide several features packaged together; for example, a single framework might supply templating, data binding, routing, and much more in a single framework. These tend to be larger, and also tend to be a somewhat more opinionated with regard to application and data structures.

User Interface frameworks, as the name implies, focus solely on the look and feel of the application by providing easy-to-use components. Most provide multiple themes that change based on the platform, and also provide mechanisms for view management. These frameworks are typically larger and much more opinionated; they often dictate file and application structure to a high degree.

Mixed frameworks essentially blend a utility framework with a UI framework. These are typically the most opinionated as the utilities and UI components are made to work together. When using a mixed framework, you'll often need to code to the framework rather than the other way around.

Most apps will use multiple utility libraries to gain specific features and will usually only use one UI framework (since these are the most apt to collide with each other and are also usually large). It's important to know, however, that though a lot of Cordova/PhoneGap apps use utility libraries and UI frameworks, you aren't required to use *any* of them; it is possible to create engaging apps without any libraries (but, it's not always easy). It's also wise to evaluate the available frameworks and determine how well each one suits the needs of your application and of your users rather than being too beholden to a specific framework.

In this chapter, we'll briefly discuss the following utility frameworks along with various architectural and design patterns:

- **AngularJS** (https://angularjs.org)
- **Ember** (http://emberjs.com)
- **Backbone.js** (http://backbonejs.org/)
- **React** (http://facebook.github.io/react/index.html)
- **Knockout.js** (http://knockoutjs.com)

The following mixed frameworks may also be of interest (UI + utility):

- **Ionic Framework** (http://ionicframework.com, based on AngularJS)
- **Sencha Touch** (http://www.sencha.com/products/touch)
- **YASMF-Next** (http://www.photokandy.com/projects/yasmf-next/, built by the author)

Let's start with some of the common architectural and design patterns used in hybrid apps, and go through the differences between some of the utility frameworks.

Common patterns

There are several patterns that you should be familiar with before we cover some of the popular platforms. We'll cover the **Model-View-Controller** (**MVC**) architecture pattern, templates, routing, and data binding.

MVC (Model-View-Controller)

MVC or Model-View-Controller is an architecture pattern that simplifies UI development. In it are many different variations, such as **MVP** (**Model-View-Presenter**) and **MVVM** (**Model-View-View-Model**), but the fundamental architecture is about the separation of concerns for easier implementation and maintainability. A simplified example of MVC is shown in the following figure:

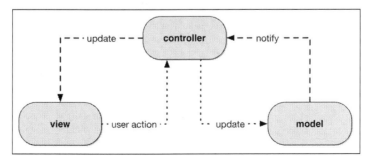

Model is responsible for storing and manipulating the data for the application: think of these as representations of the *things* in your app. For example, tasks, people, tickets, and so on.

View is responsible for displaying that data to the user. These are the physical representations of the things in your app, for example, a view might render a photograph (the view) of a person (the model). It can also act as a receiver for user interaction, but it typically doesn't act on this interaction on its own. Rather, it notifies the last piece in the puzzle: the controller.

Controller is responsible for mediating information exchange between the model and view (and *vice versa*). Should the data contained in the model change, the model notifies its controller of the change. The controller then proceeds to notify the view that it needs to update its information. Likewise, should a user change the data contained in the view or perform some other interaction (such as tapping a button), the view will send a notification to the controller. The controller will then send the appropriate changes to the model so that the underlying data structures can be maintained.

Let's assume we have a person model and a person view. The view contains an image element in the **Document Object Model** (**DOM**) that displays a photograph of the user. The view also sports a button that allows the user to take a new photograph using the device's camera.

In this context, the model might store the physical bits that represent the image, or it might only store a reference to that image. The view, on the other hand, actually makes this image visible to the user. The controller notifies the view of the information the model contains.

Now, imagine that the user taps the button to take a new picture. At this point, the model needs to be updated. The view notifies its controller that this is the case, and the controller passes the new photograph to the model.

The architecture is very simple and used in many applications. It's also been adapted and extended many times, and even though a framework might indicate that it uses MVC, it might not match the earlier shown representation exactly. In fact, it's not uncommon to see views and controllers combined together in a view controller.

Continuing with our prior example, a view controller will be responsible for both the display of the individual's photograph and for responding to the change in photograph. It communicates directly to the model in order to retrieve and set the image as necessary. This can be useful in reducing the number of files and classes, but view controllers also tend to become quite large and overgrown. Whether or not you prefer separate views and controllers or the two together is largely up to you (though some frameworks are opinionated about this).

It's also important to cover data persistence. Typically, this is implemented in one of the three locations: in the model, the controller, or the application controller, as described below:

- **Model-based persistence**: This means that the model itself is responsible for retrieving and persisting data to the backend. While this makes sense from a code perspective (the code to load and store the model is contained within the model), it also means that it's a little more difficult to test and support multiple data sources.

- **Controller-based persistence**: This means that the controller is responsible for retrieving and persisting the model. This allows a model to be stored to multiple data sources (simply by creating controllers with different data sources), but it also simplifies testing. This does, unfortunately, come at the expense of more complicated code.

- **App-controller-based persistence**: This is an extension of controller-based persistence, but moves the persistence into the application controller. The application controller is what its name indicates: it controls the entire application. It is responsible for creating controllers and providing navigation paths that the user can follow. Following this persistence pattern moves the persistence code into a single location without polluting lower controllers with persistence code, but at the expense of extra boilerplate code.

There's nothing wrong with choosing any persistence pattern you wish; in our demo app, we use the latter pattern to persist data. It has a little more code, but it comes with the benefit of the persistence layer being easily changed in one place.

The publish-subscribe pattern

The **publish-subscribe** pattern (or **pub-sub**, for short) provides a mechanism by which portions of your code can listen to events generated by other parts of your code without being highly coupled together. This allows you to write code that responds to changes in your application state without relying on the exact implementation of the other pieces. This allows for modular code whose only coupling is the name of the pub-sub channel and the data interchange format.

The DOM provides something similar, although you might not have noticed. The event model provided by the DOM operates on the pub-sub pattern: your code can subscribe to particular channels (the event), and the DOM can publish data to your code when the event is fired.

Another common implementation is message dispatch and notifications. Multiple sections of your app might register for a particular notification (say, `network-status-changed`) and react accordingly when that notification is fired (when the network goes down). Alternatively, your app's persistence layer might want to listen to notifications that indicate it should save data to the backend. When your app needs to save data, all it needs to do is fire a notification with the knowledge that another section of code will handle it appropriately.

We've already covered something similar in *Chapter 6, Application Events and Storage*, when we created a global event dispatch and handling system in order to respond to network and application-state events. As is clear from that chapter, it's not hard to write from scratch. On the other hand, there are several good utility libraries out there that implement this functionality:

- PubSubJS (`https://github.com/mroderick/PubSubJS`)
- ArbiterJS (`http://arbiterjs.com`)
- Radio.js (`http://radio.uxder.com`)
- AmplifyJS (`https://github.com/appendto/amplify`)
- Knockout
- YASMF-Next

The observables pattern

Observables are a specific form of the pub-sub pattern. They are designed to allow your code to watch other objects and to be notified when these objects change. Some libraries provide notifications if any properties on the object change, while other libraries require the observer to specify exactly which property on the object they are interested in.

This is incredibly useful, of course, as it means that a controller can watch its model and be notified when the contents of this model changes. Unfortunately, JavaScript hasn't made it easy to observe vanilla objects (though this will change with `Object.observe` support in ES7).

This doesn't mean observing objects is impossible. It's just harder (and a little hacky) to accomplish. There are two primary methods that libraries tend to use:

- Maintain a duplicate object and compare these two objects periodically, firing a notification when the change is detected.
- Specially construct an object that uses property setters to fire notifications when the property value changes (a subset of this can include libraries that modify your object for you to support this behavior.)

The first has the benefit of working with any JavaScript object you create. A huge downside is the extra memory requirement to store the duplicate as well as the performance hit from having to periodically check the two objects for differences.

The second has the benefit of being fast and doesn't use up a lot of memory at the expense of requiring the objects to be specially constructed. Some frameworks might modify the object for you, but this can be confusing. Most frameworks that use this method will simply be opinionated and require you to use their object creation methods for observing to work.

Consider the following example:

```
var task = { title: "task 1", description: "…" };
observe (task, "title", function (o) {
  // the title has changed; do something with it!
  console.log ( "Title changed to", o.title );
}
task.title = "Hello";
```

Assuming the framework has defined an observe method, the console will indicate Title changed to Hello.

Sometimes, you don't want to observe just a single property, as shown in the following code:

```
observe (task, function (o, changingProperty) {
  console.log ( changingProperty, "was updated" );
};
task.title = "Hello";
task.description = "World";
```

In the preceding example, the console will generate two messages:

```
title was updated
description was updated
```

The following libraries and frameworks provide observables:

- **Knockout** (specially created objects):
  ```
  var task = {
    title: ko.observable("task 1"),
    description: ko.observable("…")
  }
  task.title();   // returns "task 1"
  task.title.subscribe( function (newValue) {
  ```

```
    console.log ("title updated to", newValue);
  }
  task.title("task 2"; // update title; results in a log on
  the console
```

- **YASMF-Next** (specially created objects or promoted objects):

```
var task = { title: "task 1",
description: "…" };
task = _y.BaseObject.promote ( task );
task.on ("titleChanged", function ( o, notification, data ) {
  console.log ( "title changed from", data.old,
  "to", data.new );
});
task.on ("*Changed", function ( o, notification, data ) {
  console.log ( "something on the object changed" )
});
```

- **Ember** (specially constructed objects):

```
var task = Ember.Object.extend( {
  title: "task 1", description: "…"
} );
task.get("title"); // gets title
task.addObserver ( "title", function () {
  // handle change
});
task.set("title", "new task title");
```

The templates pattern

Views need to be visible to the end user. As we're using HTML, views will contain the DOM elements. Some of the biggest issues in mobile and web development revolve around how best to build views from reusable components. To resolve these issues, we use templates.

Templates are exactly what they sound like: they describe a DOM node tree in a reusable way. Placeholders for data are also indicated in the template. During rendering, the template's placeholders are filled in based on actual data, and the template's nodes are inserted in the DOM at a specific location.

Libraries that work with templates are called template engines. These engines make it easy to define and render templates and often provide a lot of additional features (such as looping over items within lists, data transformation, and more). Many large and complex frameworks will also provide their own templating engine (or are based on well known engines).

Most template engines work with string representations of HTML. A few popular engines also work with DOM representations (where the template is a hidden DOM element). Some take a different approach and make it easy to define functions that construct the desired DOM tree.

A simple string-based template might look like this:

```
"<li><span class="title">{{title}}<span><span
class="desc">{{description}}</span></li>"
```

The simplest type of templating engine supports only string substitution. The words wrapped in double braces in the example are the placeholders waiting for values. During rendering, each one is replaced by the property from a context object, essentially executing code, as follows:

```
var str ="<li><span class="title">{{title}}<span><span
class="desc">{{description}}</span></li>",
context = { title: "A task",
description: "lorem ipsum dolor et" };
str = str.replace ( "{{title}}", context.title )
        .replace ( "{{description}}", context.description);
someDOMElement.innerHTML = str;
```

If we wanted to generate a series of list items using this template, however, we'd have to go through a bit of work. In the following example, assume that render is a method that is somewhat equivalent to the preceding code, only generically:

```
// str stays the same as prior examples
var newStr = "";
var list = [ { title: "Item 1", description: "…" },
{ title: "Item 2", description: "…" },
{ title: "Item 3", description: "…" }, …];
for (var i=0, l=list.length; i<l; i++) {
  newStr += render (str, list[i]);
}
newStr = "<ul>" + newStr + "</ul>";
someDOMElement.innerHTML = newStr;
```

If you're familiar with the new **Array** methods introduced in **EcmaScript 5** (https://developer.mozilla.org/enUS/docs/Web/JavaScript/Reference/Global_Objects/Array/prototype#Methods), you can use forEach to emulate the preceding function. Alternatively, you can use reduce function:

```
var newStr = "<ul>" +
list.reduce ( function ( prev, item ) {
  return prev + render (template, item );
}, "" ) + "</ul>";
```

Advanced templating engines make it even easier to process lists. Consider this example:

```
var str = "<ul>" + "{{#foreach task in tasks }}" +
"   <li><span class="title">{{title}}<span>" +
"       <span class="desc">{{description}}</span></li>" +
"{{/foreach}}" +
"</ul>";
```

Rendering this template can then be boiled down to a single line:

```
someDOMElement.innerHTML = render( str, list );
```

There's just one problem: working with HTML in strings in JavaScript is absolutely painful. It'd be much nicer if one could work with regular HTML.

For anything more complicated than a couple of DOM elements, most template engines eschew building templates with strings. Instead, some can load an external resource and treat it as a string, or they can convert a `script` node to a string as well, both of which make it easier to work with your templates.

There's one problem, however, with many templating engines, regardless of how easy they are to work with, they often use `innerHTML`, which can often be a security risk, especially when pulling in potentially untrusted data.

Several templating engines get around this by requiring that the template exist in the DOM. This makes it easy to clone the template and insert it elsewhere in the DOM while also filling in the various placeholders in the template while avoiding `innerHTML`. While useful, it *muddies* the DOM and can sometimes interfere with other elements in the DOM.

Most templating engines add the ability to compile your templates, which also mitigates the security risk of using `innerHTML`. This converts the template strings to JavaScript that creates the equivalent DOM tree. Any of these mechanisms are enough to avoid the problems with `innerHTML`, and if your engine offers these features, it's best to use them.

Of course, one can build the DOM elements directly, but this is painful as you end up with code that looks like this:

```
var ul = document.createElement ("ul");
tasks.forEach ( function ( task ) {
  var li = document.createElement ("li");
  var spanTitle = document.createElement ( "span" );
  var spanDescription = document.createElement ( "span" );
```

```
    spanTitle.textContent = task.title;
    spanDescription.textContent = task.description;
    li.appendChild (spanTitle);
    li.appendChild (spanDescription);
    ul.appendChild (li);
} );
someElement.appendChild ( ul );
```

This is neither readable nor very maintainable. One option is to use DOMParser, which can be used in a way equivalent to innerHTML without the security risks, but this isn't available in many browsers at this time (though there is a polyfill). Another option is HTML5's template tag, but again, this isn't available in all modern browsers, and doesn't offer support for looping and transformation.

Instead, another option is to simply use a library that provides simple wrapper methods around the DOM. Consider this:

```
function renderList ( list ) {
  return h.ul (list.map ( function (item) {
    return h.li (h.el( "span.title", item.title ),
    h.el( "span.desc", item.description )
    );
  })
);
};
var list = renderList( tasks );
someElement.appendChild( list );
```

The preceding code maps nicely to HTML elements while also still being readable. It also takes advantage of native JavaScript; in that it is easy to express loops via map and other functional methods. It also avoids the security risks inherent in using innerHTML. Of course, one large downside is that it requires knowledge of JavaScript to write (which can pose a problem if you have non JS developers building your app's HTML).

The following are some utility libraries and frameworks that implement templating along with sample code so that you can see the similarities and differences:

- AngularJS:

```
<ul ng-controller="taskController">
  <li ng-repeat="task in tasks">
    <span>{{task.title}}</span>
    <span>{{task.description}}</span>
  </li>
</ul>
```

- Ember/Handlebars (`http://handlebarsjs.com`):

```
<ul>
{{#each tasks}}
  <li><span>{{title}}</span>
  <span>{{description}}</span></li>
{{/each}}
</ul>
```

- Knockout:

```
<ul>
{{each tasks}}
  <li><span>${title}</span>
  <span>${description}</span></li>
{{/each}}
</ul>
```

- YASMF-Next:

```
(function templateList ( tasks ) {
  return h.ul (
    h.forEach (tasks, function (task) {
      return h.li ( [
      h.span ( task.title ),
      h.span ( task.description )
      ] );
    } )
  };
})( tasks );
```

The data binding pattern

Data binding is pretty simple to understand: it's just tying the model to the view in such a way that when the model updates, so does the view and vice versa. It's a fast way to hook up the data to the UI without having to write a lot of boilerplate code.

Technically, there's *one-way* and *two-way* data binding. One-way data binding means that the data flows from the model to the view, but never back. You would have to add your own event listener to the view in order to respond to changes by the user. Two-way data binding means that the data flows both from the model to the view and back again. This is, of course, extremely useful, and is what most libraries and frameworks provide. The architecture boils down to this:

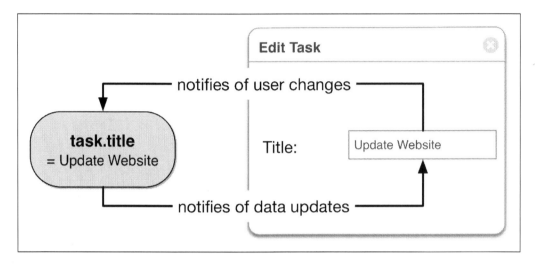

Most frameworks and templating solutions offer data binding support; the difference is usually in the details of setting things up. Often, when provided by a template engine, data binding is often wired up automatically (typically by setting an attribute in a DOM element). Let's take the example:

```
<span class="label">Task Title:</span>
<input type="text" data-bind="task.title" size=20/>
```

Alternatively, other frameworks might require you to execute some JavaScript method to wire up data binding:

```
databind( domElement, task, "title" );
```

After being rendered to the DOM, when task.title changes, the textbox will automatically get updated. Likewise, when the user changes the value of the textbox, task.title will reflect these changes.

Behind the scenes, this is fundamentally fairly simple and yet complex. At the lowest level, in order to implement data binding, one needs the ability to observe changes in the UI and in the model. The DOM makes observing changes easy:

```
el.addEventListener ("change", updateModel, false);
```

However, as we've already discovered, JavaScript doesn't provide any mechanisms to observe models. Thankfully, we can use the same techniques and frameworks that support data binding that we learned in the *Observables* section earlier in this chapter.

Here are some frameworks that support data binding and equivalent examples:

- AngularJS:
  ```
  <input type="text" size="20" ng-model="task.title"/>
  ```

- Ember (automatically updates Handlebars templates):
  ```
  <input type="text" size="20" value=title/>
  ```

- Knockout:
  ```
  <input type="text" size="20" data-bind="value: title"/>
  ```

- React (one-way; uses a domain-specific language called JSX)
  ```
  <input type="text" size="20" value="{this.props.title}"/>
  ```

- YASMF-Next:
  ```
  return h.el("input?type=text&size=20",
  {bind: { object: task, keyPath: "title" }});
  ```

The URL routing pattern

Mobile apps are extremely complex and often have a large number of views. The idea behind routing is to make managing the app and associated view states a little easier, especially with regard to dealing with history. Because Cordova/PhoneGap apps work in the browser, which is perfectly suited to maintaining history, routing can take good advantage of this. It's also useful if your development process shares code between your web app and your hybrid app, given that routing is extremely useful and popular for web apps.

Essentially, URL routing boils down to defining certain routes and associating a handler for each route. A route might be extremely simple (`/tasks`) or it might be complex and contain parameters (`/task/2/comment/12`). For each route, one or more handlers can be invoked, and these handlers are responsible for displaying the appropriate views on screen.

Although routes aren't required to use hashes, most Cordova/PhoneGap apps will as the UI tends to be rendered locally in a single page architecture app. This will look like the following code in the address bar if the address bar was visible:

```
index.html#/task/2/comment/12
```

Here is a simple example:

```
var router = new Router();
router.add ( "/task", taskListHandler );
router.add ( "/task/:taskId", taskHandler );
router.add ( "/task/:taskId/comment", commentListHandler );
router.add ( "/task/:taskId/comment/:commentId", commentHandler );
router.listen();
```

In the preceding example, the handler that most closely matches the URL route will be called. The app can then change the URL to affect changes in the view stack either by pushing new views on the stack or by popping them off (by navigating back).

Here are some libraries that support routing, along with similar examples:

- AngularJS (requires ngRoute add-on based on http://blog.hfarazm.com/angularjs-routing/):

```
yourApp.config ( ["$routeProvider",
  function (routeProvider) {
    $routeProvider
    .when ("/task",
     { templateUrl: "app/templates/tasks.html",
      controller: tasksController } );
  }
])
```

- Backbone:

```
var router = Backbone.Router.extend( {
  routes: { "task": "tasks",
  "task/:taskId": "task" },
  tasks: function () {
    // handle /task route
  },
  task: function (taskId) {
    // handle /task/:taskId
  }
};
router.navigate ("task/21");
```

- YASMF-Next:

```
var router = _y.Router;
router.addURL ( "/task", "Task List" )
  .addURL ( "/task/:taskId", "View / Edit Task" )
  .addHandler ( "/task", getTasks )
  .addHandler ( "/task/:taskId", function (v,s) {
    var taskId = v.taskId;
    showTask (taskId);
  })
  .listen();
router.navigate ("/task/21", state);
```

Presentation of the app

Now that we've covered some of the fundamental technologies of Cordova apps, let's discuss the look and feel of the app.

User Interface frameworks

Because Cordova apps use the system web view component, the look and feel of the app is completely dependent on your app's HTML, CSS, and JavaScript. Although HTML and CSS are extremely expressive and can create native feeling apps, it's true that hybrid apps don't gain many of the advantages that purely native apps do, mainly in the look and feel area.

When building a native app, one codes against the platform's native SDK. This conveys a large number of appearances and behaviors to your native app for free. Each app that uses the SDK also feels consistent; the SDK behaves the same regardless of the app on the screen.

When targeting Cordova, you are essentially trading the benefits provided by the native SDK for the benefits and perks provided by HTML and CSS. As such, your app is now responsible for the entire look and feel of your app.

Depending on the UI your app needs, this might not be so difficult, but most users expect their apps to blend in with their device's platform. The *look* of the app doesn't have to perfectly match the platform's look, but it should try to follow that platform's conventions. For example, iOS places tab bars near the bottom of the screen, while Android positions these bars near the top. Navigation bars between iOS and Android are different as well. Even with a platform-agnostic look, your app should attempt to *feel* as if it was made for the platform it is running on.

It's tempting to aim for a *pixel-perfect* appearance that perfectly matches the target platform's look and feel. However, don't do it. It's fairly easy to get to within ninety percent, but the last ten percent represent a gulf that's exceedingly difficult to cross. Failing to cross this gulf can easily land your app in the mobile *uncanny valley*—where the app looks and feels mostly like a native app, and the user will find it hard to point out exactly what isn't right—and users take it for granted to think more poorly of your app in this case. If it is clear that your app isn't aiming for a perfect duplication of the UI, your users don't have the same assumptions and don't react as badly when these assumptions fail.

None of this is easy. So, most Cordova apps will rely on a UI framework in order to take care of the look and feel. There are many good solutions available, and many pros and cons for each. It's also worth noticing that many of these frameworks can provide utility methods as well, and nearly all of them are opinionated about how your app needs to be structured. As with the utility libraries, there are a large number of frameworks available, and quite a lot of comparison has been made online. See *Appendix, User Interface Frameworks*, for links covering these discussions in order to help determine the best framework for you.

From a look and feel perspective, it certainly matters what UI framework you choose; some tend to be sluggish (especially jQuery Mobile), while others don't always follow the platform's look and feel very well. The best way to know if you like the look and feel of a particular UI framework is to try that framework's kitchen sink demo (most have them) on the mobile devices you intend on targeting. This isn't a perfect simulation of what things will be like when wrapped with Cordova, but it's pretty close. If you like what you see, then look at the various coding samples to see how you'll have to code for the framework; nearly all UI frameworks are very opinionated and have very specific ideas about how your app, its files, and its HTML should be structured.

From a developer perspective, it really doesn't matter what framework is being used, as a competent developer should be able to pick up and be productive in any UI framework quickly. The demo app in the code package is an example; it uses none of the popular frameworks, but you should still be able to understand and follow the code and see how it lines up with many of the other frameworks that are available.

From an enterprise perspective, it will be wise to balance your developer needs and the performance of the framework with what support options are available and how large the community is (which is often indicative of the available support online).

Some good UI frameworks are as follows:

- **Ionic Framework** (`http://ionicframework.com`, based on AngularJS, hybrid): This framework is quickly becoming very popular with Cordova/PhoneGap app developers. It has nice UI widgets that are modeled after their iOS and Android counterparts. A designer tool is currently available in beta.

- **Sencha Touch** (`http://www.sencha.com/products/touch`, hybrid): This framework also has an excellent reputation in the community, although it tends to be more focused on JavaScript coding than building views declaratively with HTML. There are a lot of supported themes for various platforms, though some of these are better than others. A commercial designer tool is also available.

- **Chocolate Chip UI** (`http://chocolatechip-ui.com`, requires jQuery): This framework has a very nice, nearly native UI and blends in well with iOS and Android devices. Requiring jQuery is my only demerit (I prefer that libraries avoid jQuery dependencies as it is a large framework itself).

- **Framework 7** (`http://www.idangero.us/framework7/`): This framework is for iOS 7 and 8 devices only as it aims only to replicate the modern iOS UI. Also, it does this *very well*; most users will be extremely hard pressed to tell the difference. It's completely self-contained as well.

- **Intel App Framework** (`http://app-framework-software.intel.com`): this framework has the backing of Intel (hence the name), and is becoming very popular as well. The default themes for the various platforms aren't as sharp. It includes **App Starter**, a drag-and-drop design tool (requires an XDK account).

- **YASMF-Next** (`http://www.photokandy.com/projects/yasmf-next/`, built by the author, hybrid framework): Here the author of YASMF-Next has attempted to create a small, lightweight UI and utility framework that is designed for mobile devices. It's still very young, and as such, probably not ready for production apps just yet. It's built for learning (akin to Minix from long ago), and its small code base enables coders to quickly learn concepts necessary for view management, templating, data binding, and more. As a UI framework, it focuses more on view management than the actual UI, so you'll need to provide a fair bit of CSS styles to get a suitable interface.

View management

Unless your app is a single view, you'll almost certainly need to manage your views. Most UI frameworks have mechanisms in place to do this for you, while other frameworks provide basic views that aren't opinionated in how you manage them. For example, Backbone.js provides a view class, but doesn't provide mechanisms for managing these views. It's up to you or another library. On the other hand, a UI framework like Sencha Touch or Framework 7 not only provides view classes, but they also provide methods to manage these views and determine when these views are visible and when they aren't.

If your app has one or two views, it's probably overkill to implement a framework just to manage these views, but once you add additional views, it then becomes increasingly difficult to manually control where these views are, what views they will obscure, and so on.

Most frameworks operate using the concept of a view stack. This is pretty much what it sounds like: the frameworks manage a stack of views. The view at the top of the stack is the view that is on screen, while the views below the top part of the stack are either obscured by the visible view or are otherwise off screen. In order to display a new view, you push this new view to the view stack; this usually results in an animation as one view animates off screen and the one you wanted to show animates on screen. To remove a view, it is popped off the stack, and this usually results in the appropriate animation as well.

For small mobile devices, a single view stack is probably sufficient, but larger mobile devices often display more than one view on screen at once. Since each area of the screen can navigate independently of the other, multiple view stacks are necessary.

While you don't need to know all the details of implementing a view stack if you don't want to, it is helpful to understand the various terminologies used (like push and pop). Not all frameworks use the same terminology, but they almost universally share the view stack concept.

Forms and the validation

Chances are pretty good you're already familiar with the typical form structure in HTML:

```
<form action="page/to/post/to.html" method="post">
  <fieldset>
    <label for="name">Name:</label>
    <input type="text" size=20 id="name"/>
```

```
    </fieldset>
    <input type="submit" value="Submit"/>
</form>
```

Prior versions of HTML understood the following form elements, which are still quite capable today:

- `input`, `type=text`: This enables a single line text input.

- `input`, `type=password`: This displays an obscured single line text entry suitable for passwords.

- `input`, `type=button`: This is a button with no implicit submit behavior.

- `input`, `type=checkbox`: This is a checkbox control that allows the user to toggle the control's state.

- `input`, `type=radio`: This enables a radio button defined in groups (where the value attribute is the same). Think of these like **Yes**, **No**, **Maybe** buttons.

- `input`, `type=hidden`: This provides a hidden element (the user never sees it).

- `input`, `type=file`: This is a file upload control.

- `input`, `type=image`: This is equivalent to a button, but displays an image from the source attribute.

- `input`, `type=reset`: This displays a reset button that reverts the form to the default values of the form.

- `input`, `type=submit`: This is a button that submits the form.

- `label`: This provides the label for a field; the attached input element is either contained as a child, or supplied in the form attribute.

- `fieldset`: This is a group of related fields in a form.

- `legend`: This element provides a caption for a fieldset.

- `button`: This element provides a button; this variation can include arbitrary HTML.

- `select`, `optgroup`, `option`: This element provides a list of items or a drop-down from which the user can select an item.

- `textarea`: This element enables a large text entry field.

HTML5 added many more options, and mobile devices can optimize their soft keyboards appropriately. Most of the following elements will work on many mobile browsers, but you'll want to verify their compatibility before using:

- `input, type=color`: This displays a color selector (not widely supported).
- `input, type=date`: This displays a control that allows for date selection.
- `input, type=time`: This displays a control that allows for time selection.
- `input, type=email`: Using this, mobile devices will reorder their soft keyboards to make typing @ and . easier.
- `input, type=number`: Using this, mobile devices will reorder their soft keyboard to make typing numbers easier. Desktop devices often add up/down controls to the field.
- `input, type=range`: This allows the user to enter a value using a slider or similar control. Don't use if you must have precise values.
- `input, type=search`: This enables single line text entry often styled to appear as a search field, including magnifying glass, and so on.
- `tel`: This displays a telephone dialer; mobile devices will display their dialing pad to make it easier to enter phone numbers.
- `url`: This enables mobile devices to reconfigure their soft keyboard to make it easier to type a web address.
- `meter`: This enables a meter or a gauge.
- `output`: This represents the result of a calculation.
- `progress`: This enables a progress bar.

Support for the preceding elements varies widely. Most modern desktop browsers have good support, but mobile browsers have a different story. Check `http://caniuse.com/#feat=forms` and `http://www.wufoo.com/html5/` for more information regarding support.

Of course, with data entry comes the ever important topic of data validation. The topic as a whole is out of the scope of this book, but there are a few things we need to look out for.

HTML5 brought support for form validation with no additional JavaScript libraries. Unfortunately, it has very poor mobile support, with only **Android 4.4.3** and **Blackberry** having full support at the time of writing this book. Desktop browsers fare much better, of course, but this doesn't benefit our hybrid app.

If you want to learn more about HTML5 form validation, see: `https://developer.mozilla.org/en-US/docs/Web/Guide/HTML/Forms/Data_form_validation`.

There are many good libraries available that make validation easy. Some attempt to polyfill the HTML5 form validation specification, while others provide their own API. Unfortunately, a good number of these require jQuery, which is unfortunate, as the library itself is quite hefty to include in a mobile app. If you don't mind, then you'll definitely want to pursue some of these libraries:

- Parsley (`http://parsleyjs.org`, requires jQuery)
- Verify.js (`http://verifyjs.com`, requires jQuery)
- Validate.js (`http://rickharrison.github.io/validate.js/`, no dependencies)
- HTML5 forms (`https://github.com/zoltan-dulac/html5Forms.js`, no dependencies)
- Webshim (`http://afarkas.github.io/webshim/demos/#Forms`, requires jQuery)

If your forms are simple, it's still possible (and perhaps simpler) to use typical JavaScript validation for your form.

The following are the forms and validation best practices:

- Don't rely on the browser's validation; validate the data in the backend as well.
- Do support submitting via **ENTER**; most mobile device soft keyboards will reconfigure this key to display **Go** or something similar.
- Do try to avoid long forms: mobile users shouldn't have to scroll through several pages in order to fill in a form.
- If you use placeholders in your fields, make sure it's obvious what the fields mean when data is present as the placeholder will no longer appear. If it isn't obvious, add a label to the field.
- Don't waste a lot of effort validating e-mail addresses or URLs: too many developers assume that e-mail addresses and URLs are easy to parse , they aren't. The only way to be sure an e-mail or URL is valid is to actually try and send the e-mail or open the URL.

Data visualization

Most enterprise apps will need to show some sort of graph or chart in order to make it easy for a user to grasp their data at a glance. Whether or not you need a complex charting solution or you can just get by with simpler alternatives depends largely on your users' needs and the complexity of your data.

For example, it's easy to render a simple stacked bar chart using HTML and CSS alone. Modern devices can also render **Scalable Vector Graphics** (**SVG**), which is an excellent choice to use for simple charts and graphs. You can spend time writing to the HTML5 Canvas to generate a chart, but for simple charts, this is bit overkill, and for more complex charts, you're almost certainly going to want a library that offers a lot of interactivity.

These libraries offer interactive charting and graphing along with good mobile support and performance:

- Flotr 2 (`http://www.humblesoftware.com/flotr2/index`)
- RGraph (`http://www.rgraph.net/html5-charts`)
- JSXGraph (`http://jsxgraph.uni-bayreuth.de/wp/`)
- dygraphs (`http://dygraphs.com`)
- Chart.js (`http://www.chartjs.org`)
- Sencha Touch Charts (`http://dev.sencha.com/deploy/touch-charts-rc/`)

Seeing it in action

You can find a complete and functional demonstration app that uses the presentation techniques described in this chapter (and all the other chapters in this book) in the code package for this book under the `tasker` directory. You should pay attention to the `README.md` file in this directory, as it will point out various features of interest.

Summary

In this chapter, we discussed the various fundamental patterns and presentation techniques utilized in hybrid apps, but of course, there's a lot more information than we could cover in this chapter. Be sure to take a look at the resources offered in the *Appendix*, and if you experience difficulty, the PhoneGap Google group (`https://groups.google.com/forum/#!forum/phonegap`) and Stack Overflow (`http://stackoverflow.com/questions/tagged/cordova`) are great places to get help.

Useful Resources

This appendix provides additional resources for further education and learning, which I have found useful. The resources are separated by chapter and so reflect the topics within that chapter.

Chapter 1 – PhoneGap and Enterprise Mobility

In this chapter, you are introduced to PhoneGap/Cordova and a little bit of its history. You also cover the various environments you can use to develop a Cordova app. You also briefly touch upon the application's architecture. You also will have covered the typical application structure used to create Cordova apps.

The following are important web links for reference and information on PhoneGap/Cordova:

- About Cordova/PhoneGap:
    - The Apache Cordova website: `http://cordova.apache.org`
    - The Apache Cordova documentation: `http://cordova.apache.org/docs/en/edge/index.html`
    - The Adobe PhoneGap website: `http://phonegap.com`
    - The Adobe PhoneGap documentation: `http://docs.phonegap.com/en/edge/index.html`
    - The Adobe PhoneGap build website: `https://build.phonegap.com`
    - The Adobe PhoneGap enterprise: `http://enterprise.phonegap.com`
    - The Adobe PhoneGap developer app: `http://app.phonegap.com`

- Online support groups/assistance:
  - The PhoneGap Google group: `http://groups.google.com/group/phonegap`
  - The Cordova / PhoneGap on Stack Overflow: `http://stackoverflow.com/questions/tagged/cordova`

- Useful books about Cordova/PhoneGap:
  - Shotts, Kerri. *PhoneGap 3.x Mobile Application Development Hotshot.* Second edition. Packt Publishing. May 2014. This is available at `https://www.packtpub.com/application-development/phonegap-3x-mobile-application-development-hotshot`.
  - Wargo, JM. *Apache Cordova 3 Programming.* First edition. Addison-Wesley Professional. December 2013. This is available at `http://www.johnwargobooks.com/index.php/apache-cordova-books/`.
  - Wargo, JM. *Apache Cordova API Cookbook.* July 2014 First edition. Addison-Wesley Professional. This is available at `http://www.johnwargobooks.com/index.php/apache-cordova-books/`.
  - Weyl, Estelle. *Mobile HTML5.* First edition. O'Reilly. November 2013. This is available at `http://shop.oreilly.com/product/0636920021711.do`.
  - Other PhoneGap/Cordova books available from Packt Publishing can be seen at `https://www.packtpub.com/all/?search=phonegap`.

- Developer programs:
  - The iOS developer program: `https://developer.apple.com/programs/ios/`
  - The enterprise iOS developer program: `https://developer.apple.com/programs/ios/enterprise/`
  - Android SDK: `http://developer.android.com/sdk/index.html`
  - The Windows Phone developer program: `https://dev.windowsphone.com/en-us`
  - The Blackberry development: `http://developer.blackberry.com`

Chapter 2 – Building the Data Store and Business Logic

In this chapter, you learn about the typical server architecture required for building the data store and the business logic. You also learn to design data models, writing business logic and where that logic should be placed. You also learn to design permissions and authorization models. Finally you are introduced to **Tasker**, our demonstration app.

Database servers

The following are the official links to references on various kinds of databases out there:

- Oracle: `https://www.oracle.com/database/index.html`
- MySQL: `http://www.mysql.com`
- MariaDB: `https://mariadb.org`
- PostgreSQL: `http://www.postgresql.org`
- SQL Server: `http://www.microsoft.com/en-us/server-cloud/products/sql-server`
- NoSQL servers information
  - About NoSQL: `http://en.wikipedia.org/wiki/NoSQL`
  - A list of NoSQL databases: `http://nosql-database.org`
  - Couchbase: `http://www.couchbase.com`
  - The mongoDB: `http://www.mongodb.org`

Designing Data Models

The following are links to references on data modeling tools and the Entity-Relationship model:

- The comparison of data modeling tools: `http://en.wikipedia.org/wiki/Comparison_of_data_modeling_tools`
- The Entity-Relationship model: `http://en.wikipedia.org/wiki/Entity-relationship_model`
- Data modeling: `http://en.wikipedia.org/wiki/Data_modeling`

Chapter 3 – Securing PhoneGap Apps

In this chapter, you learn the various techniques in securing your PhoneGap/Cordova app. You also learn on server specific security precautions and Cordova specific security precaution techniques.

Security resources

The following are important links to references on various security threats and practices corncerning PhoneGap/Cordova apps:

- The Cordova whitelist guide: `http://cordova.apache.org/docs/en/edge/guide_appdev_whitelist_index.md.html#Whitelist%20Guide`

- The Cordova security guide: `http://cordova.apache.org/docs/en/edge/guide_appdev_security_index.md.html#Security%20Guide`

- The Client-Side security best practices: `http://code.tutsplus.com/articles/client-side-security-best-practices--net-35677`

- Open Web Application Security Project, or OWASP: `https://www.owasp.org/index.php/Main_Page`

- The OWASP cheat sheets: `https://www.owasp.org/index.php/Cheat_Sheets`

- The OWASP XSS prevention cheat sheet: `https://www.owasp.org/index.php/XSS_(Cross_Site_Scripting)_Prevention_Cheat_Sheet`

- The OWASP SQL injection prevention cheat sheet: `https://www.owasp.org/index.php/SQL_Injection_Prevention_Cheat_Sheet`

- The OWASP HTML5 security cheat sheet: `https://www.owasp.org/index.php/HTML5_Security_Cheat_Sheet`

- The HTML5 security cheat sheet: `http://html5sec.org`

- Top overlooked security threats to Node.js web applications: `http://cdn.oreillystatic.com/en/assets/1/event/106/Top%20Overlooked%20Security%20Threats%20To%20Node_js%20Web%20Applications%20Presentation%201.pdf`

- Seven web server HTTP headers that improve web application security for free: `http://recxltd.blogspot.com/2012/03/seven-web-server-http-headers-that.html`

- Twitter's security best practices: `https://dev.twitter.com/docs/security/best-practices`

- The Passport overview (`http://passportjs.org/guide/`

- The passport authentication for Node.js applications: `http://www.sitepoint.com/passport-authentication-for-nodejs-applications/`

- 2013 Top 10 security attack vectors: `https://www.owasp.org/index.php/Top_10_2013-Top_10`

- Getting started with Passport: `http://blog.nodeknockout.com/post/66118192565/getting-started-with-passport`

- Attacks on WebView in the Android system: `http://www.cis.syr.edu/~wedu/Research/paper/webview_acsac2011.pdf`

- Keig, Andrew. *Advanced Express Web Application Development*. First edition. Packt Publishing. November 2013. This is available at `http://www.packtpub.com/advanced-express-web-application-development/book`.

- Clements, DM. *Node Cookbook*. Second edition. Packt Publishing. April 2014. This is available at `http://www.packtpub.com/node-cookbook-second-edition/book`.

- Barnes, Dominic. *Node Security*. First edition. Packt Publishing. October 2013. This is available at `http://www.packtpub.com/secure-your-node-applications-with-node-security/book`.

Chapter 4 – Building the Middle-Tier

In this chapter, you will know the reasons why it is necessary to interact with your backend database using an intermediary service. You also take a look at the middle-tier architecture, designing RESTful like API, implementing a RESTful like hypermedia API using Node.js, and handling authentication using Passport. You also learn about building API handlers.

RESTful-like API resources

The following are important links to references on REST and its features:

- HTTP methods: `http://www.w3.org/Protocols/rfc2616/rfc2616-sec9.html`

- Representational State Transfer: `http://en.wikipedia.org/wiki/Representational_state_transfer`

- RESTful HTTP methods: `http://www.restapitutorial.com/lessons/httpmethods.html`

- Hypermedia as the Engine of Application State: `http://en.wikipedia.org/wiki/HATEOAS`

- Good examples of Hypermedia APIs: `http://apievangelist. com/2014/04/15/what-are-some-good-examples-of-hypermedia-apis/`

- Passport authentication strategies: `https://github.com/jaredhanson/ passport/wiki/Strategies`

- The PAW REST client (Commercial, OS X, $19.99): `https://luckymarmot. com/paw`

- The Firefox REST client: `https://addons.mozilla.org/en-US/firefox/ addon/restclient/`

- The Chrome REST client: `https://chrome.google.com/webstore/detail/ advanced-rest-client/hgmloofddffdnphfgcellkdfbfbjeloo?hl=en-us`WizTools

- RESTClient (Java): `https://github.com/wiztools/rest-client`

Chapter 5 – Communicating between Mobile and the Middle-Tier

In this chapter, we learn about **Promises** briefly, verifying that the connection channel is secure. We learn to communicate with the backend RESTful like API and authenticating the end user with the backend.

Communication with the backend

The following are important links to references related to the backend communication:

- The XMLHttpRequest specification: `http://www.w3.org/TR/ XMLHttpRequest2/`

- The WebSockets specification: `http://dev.w3.org/html5/websockets/`

- The Promises/AP specification: `http://promisesaplus.com` and Q: `https://github.com/kriskowal/q`

- CryptoJS: `https://code.google.com/p/crypto-js/`

- Socket.IO demos: `http://socket.io/demos/chat/`

- HATEOAS JSON standards (our responses are *very* loosely based on the first item):

    ◦ The Hypertext application language: `http://stateless.co/hal_ specification.html`

    ◦ JSON-LD: `http://json-ld.org`

- Not everyone loves HATEOAS – it's good to understand why: *Why I Hate HATEOAS*. This is available at `http://jeffknupp.com/blog/2014/06/03/why-i-hate-hateoas/`

Chapter 7 – Push Notifications

Typical architecture for Push Notifications, its gateways, and setting up Push Notifications, using Boxcar, Apple, and Google Cloud Messaging, are shown in this chapter. You also will write code to send and receive Push Notifications in this chapter.

Push Notification services and BaaS

The following are important links to references on various platforms and services related to Push Notifications:

- Parse: `https://parse.com`
- Urban Airship: `http://urbanairship.com/products/mobile-app-engagement`
- Infobip Push: `https://push.infobip.com`
- Apigee: `http://apigee.com/about/`
- Appery: `http://appery.io`
- Telerik Platform: `http://www.telerik.com/platform`
- Kinvey: `http://www.kinvey.com`

Chapter 8 – Building the Presentation Tier

In this chapter, you learn the various fundamental patterns and presentation techniques utilized in hybrid apps, but of course, there's a lot more information which be could be covered in this chapter, so take a look at the following links which have references to various frameworks and libraries.

Additional utility libraries and frameworks

The following are the references and links to utility and frameworks:

- **MicroJS**: This provides a lot of small and fantastic libraries that typically only try to do one or two things. It is available at `http://microjs.com/`.

- **RactiveJS**: This provides templating, data binding, animations and more. It is available at `http://www.ractivejs.org`.

- **Rivets.JS**: small templating and data binding library, building the presentation tier. It is available at `http://rivetsjs.com`.

User Interface frameworks

The following are the links to references on the various User Interface frameworks that are currently available:

- The mobile frameworks comparison chart: `http://mobile-frameworks-comparison-chart.com`

- Comparing HTML5 mobile UI frameworks: `http://html5hub.com/comparing-html5-mobile-ui-frameworks/`

- Top 7 mobile application HTML5 frameworks: `http://www.gajotres.net/top-7-mobile-application-html5-frameworks/`

- Top 7 notable less known mobile HTML5 frameworks: `http://www.gajotres.net/top-7-notable-less-known-mobile-html5-frameworks/`

- Five best mobile web app frameworks are available at `http://moduscreate.com/5-best-mobile-web-app-frameworks-reactjs/`. Links to other frameworks are at the bottom of each article.

- Onsen UI: `http://s.onsen.io`

- Kendo UI: `http://www.telerik.com/kendo-ui`

- Ratchet: `http://goratchet.com`

- Topcoat: `http://topcoat.io`

Index

R

RactiveJS
  about 170
Radio.js
  URL 145
RAML
  URL 66
React
  URL 142
replay attack 47
RequireJS 131
REST
  references 167, 168
RESTful-like API
  Apiary 66
  cacheable 62
  client/server 62
  code-on-demand 62
  designing 61-66
  layered 62
  RAML 66
  resources 167, 168
  stateless 62
  Swagger 66
  Uniform Interface 62
RGraph
  URL 162
Rivets.JS
  URL 170

S

Scalable Vector Graphics (SVG) 162
secure communication
  ensuring 86-88
security precautions
  about 33
  authentication 41
  input, filtering 33
  input, validating 33
  output, encoding 34
  output, escaping 34
self-signed certificates
  avoiding 53
Sencha Touch
  URL 142, 157

Sencha Touch Charts
  URL 162
server architecture 18-23
server security
  backend, hardening against attack 46
  backend, securing 44-46
  Node.js with Express, settings 48, 49
session.createSession method 78
Simple Object Access Protocol (SOAP) 61
SQLCipher
  URL 58, 119, 120
SQL injection 33
SQLite
  URL 118, 120
  used, for storing local data 118-120
SQL Server
  URL 165
SSH
  configuring 44
SSLCertificateChecker 86
SSL/TLS 38
StartSSL
  URL 54
state tree 62
strict mode
  using 37
Strict-Transport-Security
  URL 39
  using 38
Swagger
  URL 66
Symantec
  URL 54

T

tags 133
Tasker 18, 165
Telerik Platform
  URL 169
templates pattern
  about 147-150
  AngularJS 150
  utility libraries 150
TLS/SSL
  using 41

Thank you for buying
PhoneGap for Enterprise

About Packt Publishing

Packt, pronounced 'packed', published its first book, *Mastering phpMyAdmin for Effective MySQL Management*, in April 2004, and subsequently continued to specialize in publishing highly focused books on specific technologies and solutions.

Our books and publications share the experiences of your fellow IT professionals in adapting and customizing today's systems, applications, and frameworks. Our solution-based books give you the knowledge and power to customize the software and technologies you're using to get the job done. Packt books are more specific and less general than the IT books you have seen in the past. Our unique business model allows us to bring you more focused information, giving you more of what you need to know, and less of what you don't.

Packt is a modern yet unique publishing company that focuses on producing quality, cutting-edge books for communities of developers, administrators, and newbies alike. For more information, please visit our website at www.packtpub.com.

About Packt Open Source

In 2010, Packt launched two new brands, Packt Open Source and Packt Enterprise, in order to continue its focus on specialization. This book is part of the Packt Open Source brand, home to books published on software built around open source licenses, and offering information to anybody from advanced developers to budding web designers. The Open Source brand also runs Packt's Open Source Royalty Scheme, by which Packt gives a royalty to each open source project about whose software a book is sold.

Writing for Packt

We welcome all inquiries from people who are interested in authoring. Book proposals should be sent to author@packtpub.com. If your book idea is still at an early stage and you would like to discuss it first before writing a formal book proposal, then please contact us; one of our commissioning editors will get in touch with you.

We're not just looking for published authors; if you have strong technical skills but no writing experience, our experienced editors can help you develop a writing career, or simply get some additional reward for your expertise.

Instant PhoneGap

ISBN: 978-1-78216-869-0   Paperback: 64 pages

Begin your journey of building amazing mobile applications using PhoneGap with the geolocation API

1. Learn something new in an Instant! A short, fast, focused guide delivering immediate results.

2. Build your first app using the geolocation API, reading the XML file, and PhoneGap.

3. Full code provided along with illustrations, images, and Cascading style sheets.

Instant PhoneGap Social App Development

ISBN: 978-1-84969-628-9   Paperback: 78 pages

Consume social network feeds and share social network content using native plugins and PhoneGap

1. Learn something new in an Instant! A short, fast, focused guide delivering immediate results.

2. This book will guide you through using the Twitter JSON API and Phonegap as a simple way to consume social media content. You'll also be able to share content to Twitter using the Twitter Web Intents.

Please check **www.PacktPub.com** for information on our titles

Printed in Great Britain
by Amazon